Honorable Heritage

Honorable Heritage

A Book of Family Folklore

Billy Boyd Lavender

HONORABLE HERITAGE
A BOOK OF FAMILY FOLKLORE

iUniverse books may be ordered through booksellers or by contacting:

iUniverse
1663 Liberty Drive
Bloomington, IN 47403
www.iuniverse.com
1-800-Authors (1-800-288-4677)

Because of the dynamic nature of the Internet, any web addresses or links contained in this book may have changed since publication and may no longer be valid. The views expressed in this work are solely those of the author and do not necessarily reflect the views of the publisher, and the publisher hereby disclaims any responsibility for them.

Any people depicted in stock imagery provided by Thinkstock are models, and such images are being used for illustrative purposes only. Certain stock imagery © Thinkstock.

ISBN: 978-1-4917-6056-7 (sc)
ISBN: 978-1-4917-6057-4 (e)

Library of Congress Control Number: 2015903545

Print information available on the last page.

iUniverse rev. date: 4/17/2015

Contents

The Football Tree

If one accepts that we descended from a single man and woman, the family tree begins with this single pair of parents at one end and widens in scope and number into the thousands. Then at some point and at some setting in the world, each of our family trees narrows back to a single pair of parents, our mother and father. In a written profile, this would produce a side view in the shape of a football. This notion would mean, of course, that we all have a common origin and are, in fact, tiny fractions of the vast whole, yet as different as individual snowflakes.

Dedication

Foreword

Honorable Heritage is an appropriate title for the following story of an honorable family. The story is intriguing; it's about family people of yesterday and today who have learned and guided themselves and others. The story is well written and well organized to show the challenging and appropriate actions of generation after generation.

Read it carefully and thoughtfully. It is exciting to read about significant people who kept going through thick and thin times, and this story can inspire each of us to be aware of the needs and opportunities around us. A book can become a guide for each of us in our thoughts, decisions, and actions. This particular book is unique; it is thorough, personal, and insightful in its depiction of the lives lived and the decisions made.

For those who remember the days of walking to school, milking cows, plowing the garden, building fires around wash pots, bathing in a tin tub, drawing water from a well, feeding chickens in the yard, slopping the hogs, canning sausage, and lighting the house with kerosene lamps, there will be moments of memory and excitement. We learned a lot, and we have come a long way.

As we read this book, we are reminded that "the strength and success of America is directly proportional to the strength of its traditional families." Our nation, states, and communities are the products of the lives of individuals and their families. We all have challenges and opportunities, and the decisions we make guide us during each phase of life. These stories may inspire us to stay positive, productive, and useful for the remaining years of our lives.

New efforts continue to be important to individuals and families. Settling into a home, beginning a job away from home, purchasing a first car, learning to play guitar, and adjusting to retirement are among the experiences that individuals and families might experience as they grow in years. There are interesting stories of "firsts" to be found in this book.

Yes, read it thoughtfully and relate to the experiences personally. We all have these phases in our journey from childhood to retirement to walking into the sunset of life. We can be grateful for the honorable heritage we have, and we have learned from the frustrations and failures we have faced. For those who are young, read the following pages and use them for guidance in the experiences to come.

—Dr. Franklin Shumake, friend and neighbor

Preface

Like a novel, narrative nonfiction imposes structure, theme, and subtext to events, places and character. Unlike novelists, authors of narrative nonfiction must live with the fact that real people and real facts seldom conform to these conventions. Reality is messy, and sometimes you have to put up with unsatisfying turns to the story.

—Edward Humes

It is impossible for anyone to write an interesting true story that has not first become history. The way the story is then presented becomes very important. The murder mystery found in *Honorable Heritage* has been challenging to present. Though the research has been thorough, research material has been limited to newspaper reports, leaving short gaps that I will try to bridge with the utmost integrity. For obvious reasons, because of those who survived the era, this story could not have been written any sooner. I hope that attempting this informative feat a century later will provide me some latitude.

My awareness of how incredibly quickly technology has advanced, changing our world, causes me to reflect upon the lives and lineage of my elderly parents. It became obvious to me during my research that the turning point in all this change came with the increased use of electricity and the combustion engine.

Each of us represents a microcosm of our common ancestry. All classes of those early ancestors who settled in America essentially acquired food, shelter, and clothing in the same manner as those who had come before them. The methods used to obtain basic needs created a much slower and more deliberately paced lifestyle than we have today. Each generation brought with it a past riddled with folklore, and each had its own historical records of origin.

The main characters in *Honorable Heritage* are related to me. Some play a more dominant role in the chronological chapters than others. However, each generation of people lived out their lives with honor on their stage of American history. Whether it was George Griffith in the French and Indian Wars of 1755, or his only son, John Griffith, of George Washington's Guards in 1780, each character had a role to play. Other key ancestors of this same era were Charles Lavender of Amherst, Virginia, and his two elder brothers, all of whom served honorably in the American Revolution.

Farther along the time line and entering the setting of *Honorable Heritage* was the Holbrook family. It was not a large family—just Frank, Lou, and my mother's grandma, Lula, their only child. Their role on history's stage was to become the victims of a sad but true murder mystery. The mystery began when eight individuals were lynched before justice could prevail. Three of the eight had been tried and were awaiting sentencing or execution; the remaining five were presumed innocent and awaiting trial. At least one of the eight was likely innocent, but that was an argument that would never come before a jury.

Other attacks—perhaps not murder, but nevertheless damaging— have come against the traditional American family over the past century. These subtle attacks on the family are not the focus of *Honorable Heritage*. However, it is my hope that, through this book, the strength of one traditional American family will be brought to the forefront. The American dream was staring each member of this family square in the face. It is also my hope that the fruits of love, keeping vows, and understanding commitments will prove attainable for others.

The conception of *Honorable Heritage* came about after I spent decades collecting genealogical records from close as well as distant relatives. Some of my materials are simple notes that I decided to jot down some years ago. I failed then to see their future significance to this work. I narrowed my focus to this title in 2010.

Ruby Neal Hardigree Lavender is the central character of *Honorable Heritage*. The scope of her life in rural America has been lived within a few miles of where she still lives today, at age ninety-six. It qualifies her as a member of the "Greatest Generation," and my interview with her was invaluable to this book.

In many American families, social class or monetary worth is not a measure of a successful life. I believe history will prove that the strength and success of America is directly proportional to the strength of its traditional families.

Acknowledgments

Different authors often need various kinds of assistance. For me, as it applies to this work, the assistance came in the form of encouragement as well as financial and technical help. In recognition of this much-needed help, I would like to thank my brother Jimmie B. Lavender and my first cousins Ronnie Hardigree and June Hardigree Dooley for providing me with constructive and encouraging criticism in addition to financial aid. Mary Ruth Moore, Millie Suttles, and Evelyn Brown are three fine, educated ladies who have helped me immensely with grammar and punctuation.

Now that I've retired from the telecommunications field, I have become more a user than a provider of technology. The technical assistance I have received from my wife, Cheryl, my granddaughter Jessie M. Guerra and Pastor Sid Fields has been much needed and appreciated as new information technologies continue to abound in the twenty-first century.

Introduction

Winston Churchill once said that a literary work should be like a woman's dress: short enough to be interesting but long enough to cover the subject. The readers of *Honorable Heritage* may feel comfortable while reading the covered subject matter. In the mind's eye, they may form a picturesque view into the lives of two families living next door to each other. The setting is in rural Georgia during the Great Depression. Watkinsville, Georgia, like every hometown community in America, has its own personal history and genealogy. The surnames of its citizens exemplify this statement, and they vary accordingly. Some people never settled in one region but popped up in another. Along with the varied surnames comes a varied history.

The basic historical facts taught in the state schools of the nineteenth century came from these pilgrims, colonists, and settlers. Consequently, the history textbooks were less than two hundred pages long, and very small—not much larger than seven by four inches, and about three-eighths of an inch thick. They included surnames of the primary settlers, which are often common names among the families living in those same communities today. The early textbooks documented the settlers' exploits with the Native Americans, and history has recorded the various types of land grants they received from our young government.

Throughout my childhood, many stories of the old days were told on the country porches of my relatives, accompanied by the fragrant breeze of honeysuckle and the late-evening songs of the whippoorwill. It's little wonder that I grew interested in and intrigued by history, genealogy, and attention to detail. In some cases, the stories provided dots along a time line that seemed to dwell in another dimension, just beyond the generation of the Great Depression. These stories—which came forth from the 1920s and 1930s with great clarity and veracity, though they were just outside my relatives' recollection—rode the winds of folklore, and the medium from which they emerged was my relatives' mothers and fathers.

One of the most intriguing stories comes from my family's recent folklore. It is the mystery of the murder of two of my direct ancestors on the farm where I grew up, and the mob lynching that followed.

Much of recent history seems more like current events, and much of it has been left out of the history textbooks entirely. In *Honorable Heritage,* it is quite permissible for the reader's imagination to ramble freely. A remarkable transition took place in the lives of my parents. One might wonder if some people living today will ever know or care how a mother and father, and millions of parents like them, raised their families through the rapid changes of the twentieth century.

At the turn of the twentieth century, much of day-to-day life was just as it had been since the founding of our country. The rapid changes brought forth by motorized automobiles, tractors, farm mechanization, and the modern marvel of electricity improved everyone's lives for the better. In 1900, the American Dream was becoming a real possibility for every citizen.

Honorable Heritage attempts to connect the way it was to the way it is. The short biographies of my mother and father represent the generation that saw it all happen.

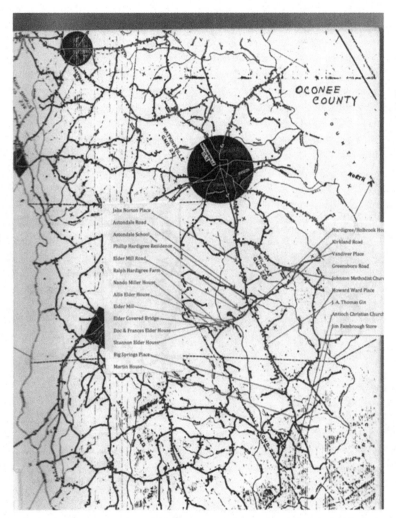

The Setting

De LaVinder, an Honorable Heritage

W esterners may ask or wonder in the twenty-first century, "How much of an American am I?" This may seem like a ludicrous question, but it rapidly branches into races of people and American principles. The question may be answered one way before the American Revolution and another way afterward. Of course, to become an American citizen, immigrants must be subjected to our immigration laws, live in this country a reasonable amount of time, and adhere to American principles. They are expected to contribute to our ideals and abide by our Constitution, and, through a legal process, they become naturalized American citizens.

Before the American Revolution, Native Americans, with their many tribal nations within the boundaries of the contiguous states, resisted adamantly the onslaught of immigrants on their country. Most of these immigrants would be classified as the "white man." They were hated by some Native Americans and loved by others, with a degree of emotional mix between the two extremes. As a result of many Indian nations, chiefs, tribes, and languages, the organizational structure was loose among them. When making deals over land, furs, and so forth, they found difficulty speaking with one voice and purpose. Many of the Native Americans were killed by warfare or disease that was brought into the country by the white man. Others were placed on a reservation, or they married into and accepted the white man's culture.

Any existing genealogical records that predate the fifteenth century either have gaps in them or are difficult to uncover to begin with. Only an extended visit overseas, aided by a great deal of luck, would allow a genealogical researcher to bridge the gaps in these records. If one is so fortunate as to map out his or her aristocratic lineage, the records become more accessible. Recently uncovered through the Sanders line, in England prior to AD 1200, was a Sir William de Ross—Knight Templar. His father was Sir Robert II, the high sheriff of Cumberland. About this same time, another direct ancestor was St. Louis IX of France. Another ancestor was the king of Jerusalem during the Crusades. However, this is not to say that the incomplete portions of any researcher's records of surnames could not hold equally shameful information about one's direct ancestry (but hopefully they would not).

In this chapter, I attempt to put the pieces of a historical and genuine genetic puzzle together. The pieces are scattered about in the Lavender surname, especially around the end of the sixteenth century. Hopefully the reader will see how these true historical facts will tell an interesting story that may seem stranger than fiction. When one traces his or her own personal ancestry back to the days of colonial immigration, he or she invariably encounters many postrevolutionary surnames. Perhaps, many decades from now, some future family member will meet this legacy with delight. Arbitrarily, all these different surnames equally contribute and constitute our makeup. I will start with the singular surname with which I am endowed, Lavender.

A noble family of Normandy, de LaVinder, whether by fate or craftiness, was able to avert the Saint Bartholomew Massacre in 1572. Protestants or Huguenots were invited to a grand party and royal feast, in celebration of the marriage of Margret a Valois to Henry of Navarre. He would later become France's King Henry IV. It was a deceitful and devious invitation, for the intent was to annihilate thousands of Protestants. After their narrow escape, the father and four sons obviously became very wary. The increased persecution of Christians in their homeland of France prompted them to leave for England.

If one adheres closely to the quotes of Emma Grey LaVinder Gorham, circa 1921 in England, they reveal, [1]"One son left for Belgium and was lost forever, so the records say. Two sons stayed in England with their father and many records were kept and William Dethick, York Herald in 1580, granted them a noble coat of arms." However, another quote from the same source gives an indication that the family may have split immediately after the massacre, [2]"Two brothers escape to England with their father, another enters Belgium, and the fourth sails for America." The descendants of the second and third brothers did not come to America until after the American Revolution had ended. Hereupon, when I use Ezra Lavender, Joe Lavender, Alan Lavender, and Thomas Lavender, it is only to suggest the strong possibility that their line is descended from the only brother that sailed in the third and final direction, America. Where and when the two LaVinder brothers separated from their father and the two remaining brothers is unknown, though it is likely they said their farewells in France.

The wars of religion, which lasted from 1560 to 1715 in Europe, were tearing France apart. Both the admiral of France, Gaspard de Coligny, and Captain Jean Ribault were Huguenots. Fifteen sixty-two became a significant year for Captain Jean Ribault. The admiral assigned the captain three ships and commissioned him to establish a colony in Florida and claim it for France. He accomplished this with the settlement of Fort Caroline near Jacksonville, Florida, much to the chagrin of the Spanish. Within this contingency plan, he was to seek out a place of settlement for the immediate relief of the persecuted Huguenots in France. To accomplish this, he sailed up the coast a short distance to Port Royal. There Captain Ribault left twenty-eight men to build a bastion, which became known as Charlesfort. In 1565,

---

[1] Halbart's Family Heritage, *The World Book of Lavenders.*
[2] Ibid.

Jean Ribault was killed by the Spanish, and Charlesfort was renamed Santa Elena. This area became a bustling port, receiving many early American shipments for the colonists. Today, this area is controlled by the US Marine Corps near Parris Island.

The first permanent settlement in America was in the Virginia Colony of Jamestown in 1608. After the Saint Bartholomew Massacre, the influx of immigrants to America greatly increased between 1572 and 1608. Though Jamestown has the distinction of being the first American port for settlers, Santa Elena in the Port Royal Sound of South Carolina has an earlier history.

In August 1572, Santa Elena was a small, struggling community with a total population of 179 settlers and 76 soldiers. The settlers were primarily farmers, who by this time were growing a variety of crops including corn, squash, melons, barley, and grapes. Livestock, including hogs, cattle, and chickens, had been introduced and were being raised with limited success.

It is a well-known fact that the attempt to eradicate Protestants in Europe caused them to begin disguising their religious identities. This could be done most effectively when they registered on a ship's manifest just prior to leaving the European ports for America. As with many other Protestant families, it is presumed that the LaVinder family changed their surname during emigration; in this case, the *LaVinder* spelling in France became the *Lavender* spelling in Jamestown or Santa Elena.

The records do not show whether the original Lavender immigrant sailed from France or England. [3]However, the first known Lavender on record in America was Thomas Lavender in 1609 in the Virginia Colony. It is quite possible that Thomas Lavender is a direct descendant of the first immigrant brother from Europe, if not the immigrant himself. Both ports of entry are significant for the time period of 1572–1608. This unknown brother who sailed to America is the one whom I claim as my direct ancestor, as the records I've studied through my investigations suggest this.

---

[3] Halbart's Family Heritage, *The World Book of Lavenders.*

If my assumption is correct, it would conveniently date him just before the earliest known immigration records. It also places the Lavender name in the earliest settlements of colonial America. In the publication *The World Book of Lavenders*, under "Lavender Immigrants," Alan Lavender of 1680 and William Lavender of 1715 are also recorded in the Virginia records. However, William Lavender, who was in Amherst, Virginia, in 1755, has been validated as my direct ancestor and is presumed to be the grandson of Alan.

Though the records have gaps for the period 1609–1715, I believe it is worth the effort to tie this immigrant LaVinder brother to all the Lavenders of Amherst, Virginia, for this period. If, in the future, the records are kind to researchers, the Thomas Lavender of Jamestown may even prove to be the LaVinder brother who sailed to America sometime after 1572.

There is only a smattering of records to fill in the span of years between 1572 and 1715. To establish some flow and continuity, I'll list these generations of sires as follows: Thomas (1608), Alan (1680), Charles (1715), William (1735), Charles (1763), Revolutionary War Record W8025, Charles Jr. (1802), William (1840, fought for Confederate States of America), Leroy (1860), Robert (1879), Clifford (1909), and Billy (1950).

James Edward Oglethorpe was born in 1696 and would later establish the Georgia Colony. The first Lavender immigrant would have arrived in America before James Edward Oglethorpe was born and ten years after Jean Ribault's establishment of Charlesfort.

The records indicate that the Lavender name had spread into the Georgia Colony by 1786, during early colonial history. This would offer a possible reason why later descendants met up with each other, possibly out of dire family necessity. It also indicates that they stayed in contact with their relatives during early colonization.

The earliest traceable and accurate records on our line of Lavenders descend from the Lavenders of Amherst. The postrevolutionary court settlement of William Lavender's estate begins this unbroken chain of information. When William died, he was in his midforties and the American Revolution had just begun. He and Mildred Mills

5

had married in 1755 and resided in Amherst. She was left with eight children, five boys and three girls, during an obviously tumultuous time in American history. Of their eight children, three of the five eldest sons had Revolutionary War records.

At the time of William's death, the children's ages were as follows: William Jr., sixteen; Winston, fourteen; Charles, almost thirteen; George, eleven; Mary, eight; Elizabeth, three; Anthony, eighteen months; and Mildred, an infant. I found it interesting that the first and last children were named after their parents.

When the American Revolution began, the three eldest boys were not old enough to fight, but in 1780, before the revolution was over, they joined the patriots. With her husband deceased and the three oldest boys at war, the remaining several years of the revolution would be difficult for Mildred and the five children.

When the war ended, the eldest son, William, was twenty-four; he married Sara Stratton the following spring. Winston was twenty-two. Charles was twenty, and he married Lucy Bellew on December 21, 1785.

When the boys came home from the war, Mildred married an opportunistic gent named William Watson. Apparently, William Lavender's mother, Elizabeth Lavender, was still alive in 1784 because she became an heir to a third of her son's estate. The younger William Lavender also inherited a third. With no husband or elder sons to support the family, Mildred had accumulated considerable debt by the time the revolution was over. Mr. Watson's position was to close out the two-hundred-acre estate, pay off her debts, and divide the balance among her children as their inheritance. This event is what gives us our court records in Amherst, Virginia.

It is not clear, but it is possible that Elizabeth passed away between 1790 and 1793, leaving her third of the estate yet to be settled. With the intrusion of William Watson into matters, the children, their mother, and their stepfather went to court for a final decree. Once the debt was settled out of Mildred's third, the court record states that the remainder of William's personal estate was to be distributed among the children and their legal representatives. It was decreed a share and share alike, according to the laws and customs of the commonwealth.

Prior to that final court decree in 1793, Charles and Lucy Bellew had two sons, Simeon Lyfus Lavender and Willis Lavender. Charles and Lucy left for Edgefield, South Carolina, to buy a farm and start a new life with their family.

On May 5, 1802, that little family would be changed forever. When the day began, Lucy had no way of knowing that one life very close to her would be taken and another very close to her would be given. While in the fields, Charles was struck and killed by lightning, and with her third child nearly due, Lucy went into labor and delivered little Charles, my direct ancestor. It was obviously a bittersweet day, leaving little doubt as to what the baby's name would be. Lucy then applied for and received a Revolutionary War Pension W8025. Then, with her two adolescent sons and toddler in tow, she sought out the Lavender families—likely looking for their assistance—first in North Carolina and then in the North Georgia settlements.

The Fort Strong and Tallassee colonies of North Georgia were expecting 127 men, women, and children. Josiah Strong and a number of hardy pioneer men preceded the colonists' 1794 arrival; he and his comrades built facilities for the coming settlement in 1786. Ezra Lavender was among these first men to arrive. Ezra does not appear in the Amherst records but was obviously a grown man by the end of the revolution. This fact introduces the possibility that Ezra grew close to Lucy's boys after her move from the Carolinas. Ezra is most likely a close relative of the Jamestown-Santa Elena group and was possibly a known relative of Charles and Lucy and others of the original Amherst, Virginia, family.

It seems apparent to me that Lucy knew her husband's relatives lived in the early north Georgia settlements. Joe Lavender was a commander of one of the local militias. Providing protection for the settlers of North Georgia from the Creek Indians was an absolute necessity. [4]"The cunning and fleet-footed Tata Nyxter and the bold,

---

[4] Wilson, *Early History*, 167.

dashing Ocean Scupeen, ranged the country in all directions; while the dreaded trio, Abe Trent, Joe Lavender and Ed Damron, were within easy reach." [5] "Johnson Josiah Strong was elected Commander in Chief, and the white men, being divided into First, Second, and Third Companies, Joe Lavender, Ed Damron, and Abe Trent, were their commanders."

In what are now Barrow, Jackson, and Oconee Counties in Georgia, the Lavender name had taken root with the aid of Ezra and Joe Lavenders' presence in those 1786 settlements. Circa 1822, Lucy and little Charles again merged into the records, obviously joining an already established Lavender family, although how close their kinship was is a matter of conjecture. Regardless, Ezra and Joe Lavender had been instrumental in settling the areas of Tallassee, Fort Yargo, Jackson, and Barrow Counties.

By now little Charles had grown up, and this region of Georgia and the rest of the South were experiencing an economic boom. He would soon marry Maria Teresa Edwards and raise a family.

The move by Lucy Bellew into this geographical area falls in line with the old Jackson County maps before it acquired new boundaries. On many occasions, I heard my aunts and uncles mention the Booth cemetery, and Uncle Carl Lavender once took some of my cousins and me on a historical trip through the region. He showed us where Great-Grandpa Leroy Lavender is buried at Prospect Methodist Church, off Tallassee Road in Jackson County. His father, William G. Lavender, and his mother, Nancy Booth Lavender, are buried in the Booth cemetery. As with so many of today's war veterans, William G. Lavender may have suffered from post-traumatic stress disorder.

Once while I was visiting my father-in-law, Bruce Anderson, in a veterans' hospital, I noticed a sign painted on a column in the lobby. It read, "The price of freedom is evident here." Throughout the rest of that day, I was cognizant of the many types of disorders that exist among our war veterans. Some of the patients, like my father-in-law, had the "thousand-mile stare" from World War II. Some veterans

---

[5] Ibid., 183.

seemed perfectly normal but wore hospital pajamas. The contrast between the two represented to me a wide range of other unseen conditions. Every generation of Americans has seen its vintage of veterans coming home from war.

As I was reading some notes on the Lavender side of the family that my cousin June Dooley had collected, I got the clear impression that William Granison Lavender, a "litter bearer" who fought for the Confederates in the Civil War, was one such traumatized veteran. One has only to imagine how witnessing the horrors of this type of work could affect anyone.

After the war, William worked in bridge construction and apparently did well at his profession. As with many war veterans, his nemesis was alcohol, which he used in an attempt to drown his memories. Because William would stop off at the taverns before he made it home with his pay, his wife assigned their son, Leroy, the task of tracking down his father in those lowly places. Leroy would pick his father's pocket and then make his way home with most of William's pay before it could be lost through this type of revelry.

Having seen what alcohol had done to his father, Leroy Lavender would not put the liquid drug to his lips. He became an avid farmer in the Jackson County area, where he accumulated significant land holdings. Leroy was a bit "out of the box" himself, as the folklore indicated he did not wear shoes in the summer. As one who can testify to how tough bare feet can become in a plowed field, I do not doubt this. Leroy and his family were prominent members of Prospect Methodist Church off Tallassee Road, now in Clarke County. Papa's father, Leroy, remarried and began having more children, so that Papa had half-siblings younger than his own children. It was time for Papa and his family to move on. For the same reasons that wagon trains went west—families and land had become crowded—Papa and Mama moved from Jackson County to the Wildcat community in Oconee County. The year was 1922, and the sharecropping opportunities were more promising there.

All the Lavenders in the Jackson County area were Methodists before Papa Lavender moved to Oconee County. After their move, Papa's children started to attend Antioch Christian Church and switched denominations in 1933. Mama and Papa followed suit in 1941. I was once under the impression that Leroy had built Prospect Methodist Church; however, during my research, I discovered in the church archives that Leroy had only donated the lumber for its construction.

The extreme eastern part of Jackson County was where the Lavenders had these significant land holdings. This farmland was within a mile or two of the Normal Town section of Athens, Georgia, near the city limits. About one mile northwest of Athens on Jefferson Road, you can make a left onto Lavender Road, which meanders back toward Tallassee Road and Prospect Methodist Church.

In February 1860, the University of Georgia purchased a site for a preparatory school in Normal Town. The outbreak of the Civil War changed those plans, however, and instead the university formed a military school. University High School was opened to train the sons of Confederate families. One of the first buildings on the school complex was Rock College, a single building constructed from local resources. Between 1866 and 1868, the state granted the school $300 annually to support crippled Confederate veterans under the age of thirty. When the funding ceased, the grounds went unoccupied until 1872. The governor of Georgia then set up a fund to assist in the restoration of the building and the construction of the State College of Agriculture and Mechanical Arts:

> [6]From 1872 to 1891 the State college of Agriculture and Mechanical Arts operated an experimental farm on this site. In 1891, the building, now known as Gilmer Hall, and 10 acres of land were deeded by the University to the State General Assembly, for the use as the State Normal School—for the training of teachers for rural schools.

In this verbose historical passage about schools and teachers, there rings a bit of truth reflected in this part of our family folklore.

---

[6] *History of the Navy Supply Corps School*

Another tale deriving from the notes that were given to June Dooley was the one about Leroy's tax indebtedness. Delinquent taxes were common among landowners after the Civil War, and so were carpetbaggers. In my imagination I had formed a mental picture of a barefooted farmer, clad in overalls, driving a team of mules to meet with Governor Gilmer to settle a tax issue. However, it may have been the other way around: the governor may have come to the university to meet with the litigants. Nevertheless, by using the few acres of land that he held in this area of Normal Town, Leroy was able to settle his tax issue. As part of what could have been an oral agreement between southern gentlemen, there may have been a trade-off in conjunction with settling Leroy's tax debt. The involvement of my great-grandfather, the country bumpkin, was unceremoniously buried, and the governor got the historical credit.

There have been several points brought forth from family folklore that indicate the possible truth of this tale. The geographic location of the Leroy Lavender estate in relationship to Normal Town is obvious. Leroy stipulated that (1) if the land was not used for continued educational purposes, it would revert back to the family; and (2) his daughters were to be trained as teachers at the state normal school. These stipulations coincide with the actual history. If the tale were not true, why would it have been told at all? The stipulations have been met by the University of Georgia and the US Navy Supply Corps School, and they are still being met today.

In the late 1980s, the Georgia Power Company purchased land and the right of way for an electrical substation construction. It netted the heirs of Leroy Memory Lavender's estate several thousand dollars each. Mother said there were more than twenty heirs.

How the University of Georgia and the Georgia General Assembly finagled the value and authorization of this land usage in 1891 is anyone's guess. The above quote from the history of the Navy Supply Corps School offers as much clarity as we have on the issue.

Robert L. ("Papa") Lavender was born to Leroy and Mary Lavender in 1879. In 1896, when Papa was seventeen years old, his younger brother, Clifford, died at the age of eleven. Papa married Bessie Mae

Sanders in 1908. A year later, Papa named his firstborn son—my dad—Clifford, after his little brother. Papa and Bessie Mae had three other children: Carl in 1912, Clarence in 1915, and Hazel in 1917.

Bessie Mae Sanders, "Mama," was tall and slender and had a dark complexion, with long, black braided hair. Mother said she remembers that women of that era had long hair, which they rolled in a bun during the day. In the evenings they would comb it out and braid it in a long plait to keep out the tangles. Bessie Mae was the youngest daughter of Mary Susan Mathews Sanders, who was the granddaughter of David Hanna Griffith.

In her later years, Mary Susan Mathews Sanders lived with Mama and Papa and the rest of their family on Elder Mill Road. When she died there in 1940, at age ninety, Mary Susan Mathews Sanders had become "Granny," the Christian matriarch of the Lavender family. She was dearly beloved and greatly respected for her wisdom. She passed away having witnessed and lived through the Civil War, the Reconstruction, the Spanish-American War, World War I, and the Great Depression.

I believe that certain traits and talents are genetically embedded in our mental and physical makeup. For example, some people are natural hunters, singers, or farmers. Hunting and fishing were two of my fondest hobbies when I was growing up in Oconee County. One day I asked my dad if the only palatable game animals were those in the hunting regulations. There seemed to be regulations for raccoons, possums, doves, quails, deer, rabbits—the list went on and on. In response to my question, Dad said that during the Depression, the springtime robins would become drunk on sour chinaberries, which made them easy to catch. He said Granny would country-fry the robins' breasts and make gravy for a meal. I tried this myself and was delightfully impressed.

Papa, Mama, Dad, Uncle Carl, Uncle Clarence, and Aunt Hazel moved into a spacious house on Barnett Shoals Road, just a mile or two from Watkinsville, Georgia. A Griffith family, kin to Mama Lavender, lived next door. About the time Papa, Mama, and the children settled into their new home, the larger Griffith family was burned out. The fire left the Griffith family literally, albeit temporarily, homeless. Papa moved out of the big house his family had just occupied and moved into an available smaller one, so the Griffiths would have a place to live. It would have been a rare deed for most men—but not for Papa, who had a heart of gold. I often heard Uncle Carl declare, "It was in his genes!"

Mama and Papa Lavender with all their grandchildren, front sitting is Bessie Mae Sanders Lavender, in her lap Jan Marie Lavender, the author standing between Mama and Papa is Billy Boyd Lavender, sitting is Robert Linton Lavender

Back row standing left to right June Hardigree Dooley, Ben Roger Lavender, Jimmie Byron Lavender and Robert Lenard Lavender, the last generation of dark hair, dark complexion, and brown eyes. (Summer of 1955)

The depression of 1920–21 is hardly mentioned in history books, as the rebound from it carved its way into the Roaring Twenties.

The trickle-down effect it had on sharecroppers in Georgia was negligible; nevertheless, it was a poor existence for the Lavender family after their move to the Wildcat community. Before Papa's farming operation could provide meat for the table, the family took advantage of the abundance of cottontail rabbits in the area by hunting and trapping them.

In 1922, when Dad was thirteen, Papa bought him a single-shot Iver Johnson .410 shotgun to use for rabbit hunting. Dad was soon invited to go hunting with the men and their dogs. After shooting and missing a time or two and being a bit slow on the draw, Dad split off from the hunters and made his way back home, where Papa asked him how the hunt had gone. Disappointedly, Dad explained what happened. Forever the optimist, Papa said, "Well, at least you got to shoot!"

Papa Lavender then set about creating an alternate strategy for harvesting rabbits. Together, Papa, Uncle Carl, and Dad built about fifty rabbit boxes for trapping. They rubbed an onion into the wood around the entrance to each box, hoping rabbits would be enticed by the smell and hop inside, triggering the doors to close behind them. They discovered that once a rabbit had been caught in a box, its scent permeated the wood, making for more successful trapping. To bring all the boxes up to that standard, a rabbit's bladder was salvaged from the dressing process and successfully used for bait.

Before school each morning, Dad and Uncle Carl would mount their mules and check about twenty-five boxes each, putting their catch in their cotton-picking sacks. On a good morning, they would clean more rabbits than the family needed. The extras would be taken to Watkinsville before school and sold to the public for a quarter apiece.

That same year, the Astondale School burned, and a new, red-brick schoolhouse took its place in Watkinsville. The county's children between ages six and sixteen were schooled there. After Uncle Carl and Dad finished the eleventh grade, Papa decided that it was important for them to learn a trade, and he enrolled them in the Monroe Agricultural and Mechanical School. To help pay his way through school, Dad chose to sell Bibles on commission in the Appalachian foothills. From that experience comes the following tale.

It must have been in 1925, when school was out for the summer, that my dad took the job selling Bibles. Somewhere near Knoxville, Tennessee, the book company representative gave Dad his instructions, told Dad where to meet him in three days, and then left Dad on foot, book satchel in hand, to go from door to door among the mountain people.

The road where Dad was left narrowed as he walked along, until it became a path. It was getting late in the afternoon when he saw a cabin in the distance. As soon as he saw it, a man stepped onto the front porch with a shotgun and shouted, "Don't come any closer!" Dad raised the Bible to show his purpose for being there and that he meant no harm. He stepped closer so he could be seen clearly, and the man let down his guard and invited him onto his porch. The man ordered a Bible and then apologized for his abrupt greeting. "Son, we make corn liquor in these parts," he explained, "and we hung a revenuer last week, in the next hollow, so things are tense around here." The man called his two sons to his side, and they stood in a huddle, murmuring about what to do with Dad. By this time, Dad was feeling the pressure.

Hungry and scared, Dad was taken by the sons down another long path to a mountain stream, where they stopped and rested for a while. One of the young men pulled a brown jug from under a rock in the cold stream and passed it around. Dad partook and passed it back. Their attitudes toward each other quickly turned from duress into a warm tingle of cordiality. After a couple of rounds, as the pressure eased, but before too much damage was done, the two young men pointed out the direction Dad should go and adamantly said, "Don't come back!" After a couple more rounds, Dad passed out. The next morning, he woke up by the stream, with the satchel and sample Bible under his head for a pillow. He shook the cobwebs from his head and started walking again.

Taking the advice of the young men, he didn't even look back. He walked until he came to another road, took it, and continued to walk until early evening, without a house in sight. Humbled to the bone and nearly starving, he came upon another cabin. He stood in front of the cabin and called out, and a lady emerged. He explained his situation, and as politely as he knew how, he asked if she had anything for him to eat. She replied in a direct manner, "Wash up and sit here on the steps until I call you." Some time passed before he was called inside. There on the table was a large bowl of fried okra, freshly prepared. Dad later told me that was all that she offered, but he was glad to get it.

Once when Dad and I were planting the garden, he commented, "If your mother didn't like okra so much, I wouldn't plant any at all." When I asked why, he remarked, "Well, it's a curious plant. The seeds are hard to germinate, and then when it finally does sprout, it will grow up over your head."

"Is that the only reason?" I asked. Then came the Bible story from his time in the mountains, and that's when I got it.

In the twenty-first century, vocational technical schools are still providing adequate education for those willing to apply themselves to their profession. At Monroe A & M, Dad and Uncle Carl learned carpentry and mechanics and became skilled in both. Throughout his life, part-time contract jobs allowed Dad to do what he loved most, and that was to farm. As farming methods improved, he and Uncle Carl were some of the first farmers in Oconee County to take advantage of them. I have seen Dad rebuild his tractor engine under a walnut tree in the backyard. He would remove the engine head to replace the rings and piston sleeves, and then, using a borrowed chain hoist, he would pull the engine block up on a strong tree limb. It was all over my head—no pun intended—but Dad could explain every step of the process, down to the timing and compression stroke.

Masonry is one skill at which Uncle Carl and Dad were equally proficient. I never saw them lay bricks, but I helped them lay hundreds, if not thousands, of cinderblocks. Mixing the mud was my job. It was called "mud" for short, but it was actually fine-quality sand mixed with cement to form the mortar. Too much water and it became runny; too little and it became too stiff to use. Several cinderblock buildings that they built are still being used in Watkinsville today. They built Hot Thomas's BBQ and the cottonseed facility next door (now a public meeting hall), two tenant houses for Uncle Carl, and several other cinderblock homes. Mama Cleo Hardigree was provided a nice cinderblock home in Watkinsville, near the home of Uncle Thomas Hardigree. And when Mama and Papa Lavender became older, Dad and Uncle Carl built an addition to Uncle Jerry's house, where many Sunday afternoon visits culminated. The list of Dad's building projects goes on, but it was obvious to me that his first love was farming, so I asked him how that came about.

To my surprise, his voice cracked as he told me the exact moment he fell in love with farming. He was a small boy, maybe four or five years old, plowing in a field with Papa Lavender. Papa would put Dad in his lap while they plowed a two-mule, two-disk plow, turning the earth together. "The rich smell of turned earth got into my soul," Dad said with emotion.

In Dad's later years, he and Mother would travel hundreds, if not thousands, of miles to the Delta farmlands on the Gulf of Mexico. They would also travel north to the seemingly infinite cornfields of Wisconsin, marveling with intense pleasure at the ways and means of modern farming.

However, from 1927 forward, putting a crop in the ground and harvesting it with mules was the order of the day for Papa, Clifford, and Uncle Carl. Papa's farming success coincided with the growth of his two eldest sons. About 1927, Papa and Mama moved from Barnett Shoals Road near Watkinsville to the Martin house off Greensboro Road, seven miles south of Watkinsville. Dad was eighteen, and Uncle Carl was fifteen. There they sharecropped with Phillip Hardigree for two growing seasons. Jim Fambrough's store became their local meeting place for news and information after a hard day's work. Their home, the Martin house, was just up the road, and Papa and the boys would take the wagon and mules home for the evening. Their late-afternoon meetings put Uncle Carl in the Fambrough family's neck of the woods, where he later met and married Jim's niece, Lizzie Ruth Fambrough.

While Papa and Mama were still living in the Martin house, they learned about another opportunity to sharecrop, with John Clovis Saxon. His land was located closer to Elder's Mill and the Covered Bridge area. This became an amenable partnership for the next several years, and it brought the Hardigree and Lavender families together as next-door neighbors on Elder Mill Road. This became the setting for much of the following text. Mother and Dad lived and died within a five-mile radius of these two houses.

Dad's Bible

A Cherokee in the Woodpile

❧ ———— ❧

I remember the day as clearly as if it were yesterday, but actually the years have flown by since that warm spring day in the late 1960s. It had to be early to midspring, because my dad and I were hoeing the garden and the plants were bursting forth with foliage. My three older brothers had already left the nest. I was about to do the same, but until then, Dad and I worked closely together. I was the baby boy, and by then my parents had finished rearing the previous three, so they had the process down; they had learned to utilize my help with maximum efficiency. After attending school each day, I milked five cows, slopped two hogs, used two five-gallon buckets to feed ten thousand chickens, and did a host of other daily chores. There was little time left for frolicking and entertainment, so we humored ourselves in conversation as we worked.

Though Dad was sixty years old when I left home, he was still quite a man. He was almost six feet tall and seldom weighed less than 210 pounds, and he was hardened from a lifetime of physical labor. His muscles were like hard rubber. His hands were not always gentle, but when he drew you into his arms, close enough for you to feel the dampness of the day-old sweat in his overalls, you knew a real man was hugging you. He always impressed upon his sons the importance of giving a man a firm handshake. In later years, his doctors and

20

surgeons would wince when he shook their hands, but they never forgot the name of the man standing in front of them.

On this particular spring day, I leaned back on the hoe handle and asked him a question that had been burning inside me for quite a while. "Dad, where did we get the Indian blood?"

Dad had high cheekbones and a dark complexion, and all four of us boys had skin almost as dark as his. By the first week of spring, the five of us already had farmers' tans; by the end of summer, we were brown as ginger cakes. Dad stopped and rested on his hoe handle. "What little Indian blood we have comes from Granny's side of the family."

"What kind of Indian was she?" I asked.

"Granny was of Cherokee heritage," he said.

Beyond that little bit of information, the subject was almost taboo. Dad's response also indicates to me that Granny would have been the only true source for that type of information. I knew the discussion was over when I told Dad that I wanted to research our family tree. He chuckled and told me to be careful—he'd heard of a man who researched his family tree and found out his great-grandfather was a horse thief who had been hanged by the neck in the county square. But that just made the subject all the more intriguing to me.

From all the family folklore and stories I'd heard told on the front porches of my relatives, I had become acquainted with my ancestry in a special way, and I had a fair knowledge of our origin. But the dark-eyes-and-skin characteristic of those of my generation and earlier generations indicated that somewhere, someone had injected dominant genes into the family tree. My cousins, my uncles and aunts, and our grandmother all bore the same genetic features: dark eyebrows, brown eyes, and a dark complexion. Some black-and-white family photos were passed along to me, and while it's difficult to distinguish skin tone, the dark eyebrows and high cheekbones are prevalent.

Ironically, all my children and my first cousins' children, from Granny's side forward, had the recessive blue eyes. They also had fair complexions and, in some cases, blond hair. This shift occurred in a single generation; the Cherokee genetic dominance seems to have waned.

Some of my adult relatives who also studied family genealogy discovered I had an aspiration for writing and sent me some clippings from the history book *Our Kin*, on the Griffith line. This really set the wheels in my head to turning. Dad said that Granny was kin to the Griffiths way back, all the way to the French and Indian Wars in 1755, and to Wales in the United Kingdom.

Granny was the topic of many stories about the good old days. She was the family matriarch, born twelve years before the Civil War. She had marveled at the invention of the radio, and she would tell her twentieth-century grandchildren not to be so loud in the house because the people on the radio might hear them. In the early years of radio, that sort of reciprocal operation was not possible, but in today's world she would not have been far off the mark with her observation.

Because of Dad's input about Granny's heritage, I started my research on the years prior to 1849. I felt that nineteenth-century southerners would have shunned the marriage of a Caucasian to a Native American, so my sense of intrigue deepened.

The records prior to 1825 indicated that Granny's father, Coleman T. Matthews, was a landowner in Oglethorpe County, near Echols Mill in Lexington, Georgia. He married Sara Ann Griffith. Considering the history of the Trail or Tears, it does not seem likely that Coleman T. Matthews was of Cherokee heritage, but this possibility cannot be ruled out. The question that arose for me was this: How many Cherokee Indians would have had substantial land holdings, such as the property my ancestors held, in 1825? Another obvious question would be, How dominant would Native American genetics actually be, had they descended from further back in history? Would those dominant physical features still carry over four or five generations into the twentieth century if a pure genetic insertion had not occurred early in the nineteenth century?

Wondering about the strength of dominant Native American genes and their carryover from early in American history, I happened upon the research of Laura Beth Duffy on Native American genealogy. She describes the way genetic traits manifested themselves into the twentieth century. Of the five major diseases that surfaced, I had them all. Two of them are diabetes and heart disease. Also other, smaller traits such as characteristic eye color, skin pigmentation, and teeth, and so forth are still detectable. Keeping my focus on how these Native American genetics might have entered our family tree, I discovered only one possibility, which surfaced from the writings of our family descendants in the book *Our Kin.* The tale dates back to the French and Indian Wars of 1755.

Lieutenant George Washington and General Edward Braddock apparently met in conference one fateful day in 1755 during the French and Indian Wars. Before the march on Fort Duquesne, Washington served as a scout under the Crown of England, and on this day he presented to Braddock his scouting report for the march. The bastion was heavily fortified inside and out. Large numbers of Native Americans—French allies—lay along the trails to Fort Duquesne. Braddock ignored Washington's report that the Native Americans were planning an ambush along these wooded trails; the march went on. Eight hundred loyalists were killed on the day of Braddock's Defeat in 1755. Only by the miracle of a literal smokescreen (created by the explosions of black gunpowder, mixed with fog and dust in the mayhem) did our first president avoid disaster. Slain on the trail was George Griffith—a pioneer leader and militiaman, and the father of a young boy named John, his only son.

John Griffith, born in 1744, was only eleven years old when Braddock's Defeat occurred. Sometime afterward, he received his father's powder horn and British sword. John Griffith continued to follow George Washington as the Continental Army was formed; he became a patriot and, later, a member of Washington's Guards.

General Washington formed Washington's Guards during the early days of the American Revolution, in 1775, to serve as an elite force that would surround him as his personal aides. John Griffith was a member of this 250-man roster and one of the first to wear the American military uniform. One of Washington's requirements for his guards was for them to have fought in all his battles.

By October 1780, John Griffith was thirty-six years old and living in North Carolina with his wife, Ann, and their five children. He had finished his enlistment with Washington's Guards, but the revolution had not ended; he was called back into service at the Battle of Kings Mountain in North Carolina.

One historical account indicated that John and Ann had moved to Oglethorpe County, Georgia, after his enlistment was up, but he was called back into service from there when the war seemed to be going badly. [7]His name was last borne on the muster roll for October 1779, dated at headquarters November 1779, at the end of his enlistment. He was called back into service for the Battle of Kings Mountain in October of 1780. He most likely was still living in North Carolina eleven months after his hitch was up when called back into service.

> [8]John was one of the first to respond. One morning in October, just as the sun was peeping over the eastern horizon, the news came that Col. Ferguson's troops were advancing to give battle on Kings Mountain in North Carolina. The brave John Griffith was among the foremost, and later in the fight was seen in deadly combat with a British officer.

> My research uncovered a significant fact: Colonel Ferguson was the only true Briton in the fight. He commanded all the other combatants, who were American-born Tories, or loyalists, fighting against the American patriots.

Just before the British retreat, John was run through with the British officer's sword.

Having lost his fight with the Tory by the narrowest of margins, Griffith's life was spared. As was usually the case in this type of

---

[7] Griffiths, *Our Kin*, 1052.
[8] Ibid., 1060.

warfare, at the close of the battle, the ground lay strewn with dead and dying men. [9]"His life was saved by Mr. Carruth, who, finding him lying on the ground, turned him on his side so that the wound would drain, thus preventing his being poisoned by gangrene." John Griffith was very critically wounded.

In modern warfare, soldiers can be evacuated from the battlefield by helicopter within minutes of being wounded, thus increasing their chances of survival. In 1780, however, an injured patriot had to hope for sympathy from other patriot families. The Battle of Kings Mountain was fought just west of the Catawba Basin in North Carolina. The rural homes scattered about were the best hospitals available. This area of North Carolina was still heavily populated with Catawba and Cherokee Native Americans, who by now had seen the inevitable outcome of the revolution. Some had already started a migration westward on a trek that later became known as the Trail of Tears. [10]The facts become sketchy at this point, but it is believed that a woman named Hanna took John Griffith into her home, giving him her bed. She instructed that two Tories be laid on the floor.

Thus far, I have not been able to reach a satisfying conclusion in my research of the dominant genetic influence of Native Americans in my family. As the records indicate, David Hanna Griffith was already an unnamed infant in North Carolina when the Battle of Kings Mountain occurred. He was the sixth of seven children. However, under the circumstances, this seems the only logical time when these dominant genes could have been inserted into our family tree. Nowhere else in the records is there an indication of such a genetic insertion, or even the likelihood of one, on Granny's side of the family. I can provide no proof of the following theory, but Hanna, possibly a Caucasian midwife, could have been unwittingly caring for an orphaned Native infant during this interim period. Only one child is in question. A natural bond could have developed between

[9] Ibid., 1052.
[10] Ibid., 1060.

this orphaned papoose, John, Ann, and Hanna during John's slow rehabilitation process. Did the fruits of convalescence far outweigh any tone of racism, with love becoming its greatest virtue?

I suggest that when Ann did arrive at Hanna's home, she assisted Hanna there until John was well enough to travel. This may have taken months. The image of Ann and the baby on horseback, arriving at Hanna's home is a powerful one and could have occurred on several occasions as John rehabilitated.

I suggest that a full-blooded Native American at this time in our family tree could inject enough dominance into his progeny to last a hundred and fifty years and manifest itself in my generation. This occurrence had to have happened at a time when the dominant physical traits could have carried over into the twentieth century. A genetic package created by infidelity seems out of the question, since the strength of that genetic package would have only been half. If this indeed was the era when the genetic insertion occurred, I would also suggest that it occurred under the most honorable of conditions.

This is a tale of patriotism, combat in war, and personal sacrifice. It speaks of a father's love for his family and his country. It is about the birth of a nation and the birth of a child. It is a tale of how the names of four individuals were presented on the grand stage of history for future generations to analyze. Whatever the case, this tale is written to suggest that the moral high ground was taken by the responsible parties in 1780.

Ann heard of her husband's condition and where he might be found. She apparently thought the distance between them was not too far to travel on horseback. One thing may have kept her from going to John's bedside immediately: she had five other young children in her care. This may have been the obstacle to her departure. She obviously would have had to make arrangements for the care of the other five children during her absence, and the baby in question likely was not yet weaned and would need its mother or a wet nurse nearby. [11]"John gave his hostess such an accurate account of Ann,

---

[11] Ibid.

that when she rode up to the gate, his hostess looked out and said, 'John, Ann has come.'" In this account of their reunion, there is no mention of a baby.

One researcher notes,

> [12]David Hanna Griffith was given a piece of land by his father, which is on record in Oglethorpe County, and called him David Hanna. I somehow feel that this "Hanna" was added to his name when he was a baby and very probably for the lady who nursed his father, John Griffith, back to health when he was wounded at the Battle of Kings Mountain, but the researcher could find no proof of this. On one of the oldest DAR papers on this particular son, it is told how his mother carried him on horseback to visit the wounded man.

The scene of Ann and the baby arriving on horseback at Hanna's location, taken from the DAR records, automatically makes the argument for the baby's relationship to the family. That theory thus became a documented fact. Ann most likely did not stay over for long periods of time at Hanna's and commuted back and forth, carrying the nine-month-old Native American with her on some trips. She most likely transited most of the distance between their homes by buggy or stagecoach and only used a horse for the short distance over the more rugged terrain.

Toward the end of my research on this matter, I achieved as much closure as I ever would when I read a statement given by John Griffith to his family on his inheritance matters. Regrettably, the statement is now only a part of my memory; I have not been able to relocate it for footnoting. But, effectively, it stated that David Hanna was to receive an equal part "the same as any other child," or similar wording. This would indicate that John was aware of how messy inheritance issues

---

[12] Ibid., 1402.

could become, and that he included the statement for clarification because there was something different about David Hanna.

[13]Sometime after his rehabilitation, John received 3,315 acres in land grants for his patriotic sacrifice, and the family moved into the Oglethorpe County region of Georgia. Is it possible that Ann and John found it easier not to explain the adoption of a Native infant to anyone at this critical stage of promissory land grants, of which John was a significant recipient?

In the future, through the wonders of DNA, we might be able to find more information on David Hanna and the possibility of his Native American heritage; I welcome that challenge to my supposition. Could this mystic have been rooted in the mind of four-year-old Mary Susan Mathews in Clarke County, Georgia, who became Granny, as she peered into the casket of her grandfather, David Hanna Griffith, in 1853? Could she have seen and carried with her all the genetic traits of this dark and handsome patriarch, who was unwittingly orphaned into Hanna's care just before the Battle of Kings Mountain during the American Revolution?

---

[13] Ibid.,1052.

Bessie Mae and Granny

The Handsome and Haunting

꒰ꙫ꒱ ──── ꒰ꙫ꒱

It was a cold and windy day in November 1966. Dad used his Allis-Chalmers WD tractor to twist and back the load of corn up to the crib. It gave the appearance of being jackknifed on the narrow dirt road, but actually it wasn't. At what is now Kirkland Road, near the intersection of Highway 15, Dad and I worked hurriedly to offload the corn into the crib so we could clear the dirt road of its obstruction. It was on this occasion that the true origin of what was now a corncrib came to light. I could remember a half-dozen such small frame buildings, as well as a few larger barns scattered around the farm, that we had removed as eyesores, salvaging the lumber. [14]Dad explained that this corncrib had been part of the Holbrook store and annex where, on May 9, 1905, my mother's great-grandparents were savagely murdered. The forty-one-acre tract of land on which it sat came into the family's possession when Francis Marion Holbrook and Louisa Hill (Lou) Holbrook purchased it from the Astondale estate circa 1900.

I consider myself particularly blessed, as 66 percent of the surnames in my ancestry can be traced to the time of the American Revolution and prior. For many Americans, "immigration" was something that happened to their parents or grandparents. Then

---

[14] "Aged Man and his Wife Murdered Near Athens," *Atlanta Journal*, May 11, 1905.

a narrower migration occurred, from state to state or county to county, taking them in the direction of prosperity and the pursuit of happiness. My immediate family moved around within Oconee County quite a bit prior to 1950 when the Holbrook house became available for us to rent from Mother's grandfather, Phillip Hardigree.

I'm truly blessed by having been raised in one family, with one mother and father, in one house in the same county and state, after 1950. [15]Phillip Hardigree's in-laws, F. M. and Lou Hill Holbrook, moved to Oconee County from Banks County in 1901. They acquired this farm and farmhouse with annexed buildings at the location where Mother now lives on the original Astondale estate. It's not clear whether the Holbrooks were in the mercantile business in Banks County before moving to Oconee, but by 1905 they were doing well at their new location, in the house and store annex near the corner of Greensboro and Kirkland Roads.

In those days, sharecropping was common, and sharecroppers' frame houses were scattered throughout the countryside of rural Oconee County, Georgia. [16]It was a time before motorized transportation, so walking, bicycles, mules, horses, buggies, and wagons were the predominant means of travel. For the local transients, these slower forms of transportation provided a quieter and closer look into the stores and homes, and thus the lives, of the people living along the road.

Most of the black families in that area retained the last names of slave owners. Taking those names was, long ago, a convenient way of identifying groups and kindred black people. In the 1950s and '60s in the Deep South, many black families still had not moved from the countryside into the townships. But as their frame dwellings fell into disrepair, that transition hastened, leaving a predominantly white rural county. In 1905, however, south Oconee County had

---

[15] Ibid., "The Store was Ransacked," May 11, 1905.
[16] Ibid., "Three are Arrested for Double Murder," May 11, 1905.

a moderate number of black families carrying white surnames—Willoughby, Elder, Robinson, Fambrough, and so forth—from early settlers.

At the turn of the twentieth century, two different secondary dirt roads intersected the main dirt road, now Highway 15. The store annex was located at the corner of Greensboro Road and Kirkland Road. Now paved, Elder Mill Road and Kirkland Road intersect Highway 15 at the same point they have since their dusty origin many years ago. This was the setting of the double murders in 1905. As a small boy playing under the walnut trees in the backyard, I can remember Dad using a mule to plow up potatoes just yards from where the house and store annex would have been.

After the double murders of F. M. and Lou, the initial corner tract of forty-one acres formed by the intersection came into the possession of Phillip Hardigree and Lula Holbrook. The well for the store annex left a sunken hole within ten feet of where my mother's satellite dish is anchored today. It is believed the well was accessed from the porch. The porch of the store annex became the setting for the most gruesome double murder in Oconee County's history.

[17]The second day after the murders, the *Atlanta Journal* reported, "Mr. Holbrook had one child, Mrs. Phillip Hardigree, Lula, who lived half a mile from them and who spent the day before the murder with her mother. [18]She said that she was thankful that their bodies had not been burned in the house." This suggestion, that a fire had been extinguished, gives credence to speculation that the murderers left the lanterns lit after plundering the house and ransacking the store. It will never be known why the bodies were dragged onto the porch. Maybe an unknown witness made a feeble attempt to save them before the annex blaze was stifled.

[19]The farmhouse-store annex could have previously belonged to Lou Holbrook's sister, Carrie Hill, who had a millinery store at the same location. It's not clear why F. M. and Lou left Banks County.

---

[17] Ibid., "The Store was Ransacked," May 11, 1905.
[18] Ibid.
[19] Ibid.

One likely possibility is that the proceeds from a lawsuit in Banks County afforded them an opportunity to start afresh on that tract of land. Between 1901 and May 9, 1905, their business prospered, and as it was noted in the *Atlanta Journal,* [20]"about ten days prior to the murders he deposited $900 in the bank in Athens." This deposit was believed to have been from the settlement in Banks County.

Several species of trees are scattered about the farm. Among the variety of trees are a holly, crabapple, elm, and black walnut, and at one time there was a big cedar right in front of the house, along the road. I am not sure how many of these trees were set there by my great-grandpa Phillip. Some of the trees predate the turn of the twentieth century; they were set out during the Holbrook occupation. Phillip built some of the outbuildings—*that* I remember. There were two frame structures that I remember well as being part of the Holbrook farmhouse-store annex. One was the previously mentioned corncrib, and the other was, in fact, a store. Both were moved away from the damaged annex after the murders, for a different use.

The store portion was moved closer to Greensboro Road; it still contained items from the Holbrook annex. It was still there in 1950, along with seven or eight other barns and outbuildings needed to run the farm. The store always seemed out of character for Great-Grandpa Phillip, but now it seems it had its purpose in depleting the vast array of items he needed to sell after the estate sale immediately following the murders. His modest venture into the mercantile business was simply a means of dispensing of the items from the Holbrook store.

The structure where the murders occurred was deliberately demolished soon after the crime. Our large white house was built after the murders, between 1906 and 1908. It still sits adjacent to the corner formed by the intersection of those primary and secondary roads. Mother has lived there for the past sixty-four years. Ironically, the house is in much better shape now than it was in 1950, when our family of six moved into it. To my knowledge, it had never been

---

[20] Ibid., "Bodies Sadly Mutilated," May 11, 1905.

painted, and its newness had long since been lost when we moved into it forty-two years after its construction. The entire house was built from heart pine. Some of the knots from the tongue-in-groove flooring had released from the wood, leaving perfectly round holes through which chickens could be seen dusting beneath the house. Someone used lids from opened cans to seal the holes. After Phillip Hardigree died in 1960, we were able to purchase the house and the surrounding forty-one acres from the rest of the family. In 1961, Dad switched from row cropping to poultry farming, and we started the repairs on the Holbrook-Hardigree house in earnest.

It was such a drastic makeover, in fact, that I won the Future Farmers of America State Home Improvement Award in 1965. The award came with a trip to the National FFA convention in Kansas City, Missouri. Not one square inch of the Holbrook house exists that I have not opened up a door and peered at, or covered with a paintbrush. One of my observations came from the roof over the kitchen area, where the wood stove flue came through the shingles and some honeybees had made a home in the old, unused flue. This was the origin of an oozing, smutty syrup that would drip into the kitchen on hot summer days. Not until the red-brick flue was completely removed was the problem solved. Not often does a teenager find himself on the roof of his home, but on this rare occasion, I saw some numbers etched in the base mortar of the beehive flue: 1908. Oftentimes when construction of a building was nearing completion, a date would be scratched into the soft mortar before it hardened.

As an adolescent growing up in the Hardigree-Holbrook home, three old pictures seemed more creepy than interesting to me. Now that I am older, those heirlooms are invaluable—not monetarily but educationally, providing more dots on that time line to the other dimension just before the Great Depression and during the Reconstruction period. The people whose photographs hung on the bedroom walls—one was a family portrait with a small boy—were believed to be members of the same family. No names are written on the backs of the two adult portraits. Mother and other family members identified the people in an oval, beveled-glass frame as Ralph Hardigree Sr. at age four in 1899; his mother, Lula; and her parents, Lou and Frank Holbrook. Frank apparently played the fiddle, at least well enough to want it in the picture with him. In the background is an old frame house that I could not identify as a local house while I was growing up, so I asked Mother about it. She cleared up my confusion by saying, "The picture was made in Banks County before they came to Oconee County." My grandfather is in the middle, and Lou Hill Holbrook is on his left. The picture is elaborately encased in that oval, beveled-glass frame, which gives it the appearance of being a rare antique.

The other two photos are eighteen-by-twenty-two-inch portraits of two strikingly handsome, well-dressed people. The man is in late-nineteenth-century attire, and the woman—apparently his mate—is dressed likewise. Each of the portraits is in its own frame, made in the same era as when the photos were made. Over the years, I must have asked the same question more than a dozen times: "Who are these folks?" And I got the same answer: "Those are the Holbrooks. Those pictures came with the house."

The photos stirred much interest among the rest of my relatives, whose many questions about them could never be answered sufficiently. In an effort to hide them, Mother tucked them in their frames behind false fronts, but she left the oval one with Grandpa Ralph hanging in her bedroom.

The Holbrooks

The Holbrook house was built in 1908. It is a big house but not necessarily large. There are more than a half-dozen closets, a large kitchen, a dining room, and four bedrooms, one of which is Mother's bedroom today. It is the same bedroom where her Grandmother Lula lay in state in 1927. It is adjacent to a large breezeway/hallway with front and back entrances and a staircase leading to a large upstairs bedroom. The upstairs is where my brother Bobby and I spent our late teens and young-adult years. The two handsome and haunting pictures of the man and woman were tucked in the upstairs closet by my bed for a while. Every time Bob and I opened the closet door, we would see them. I suppose because I asked more questions about them than anyone else did, Mother has agreed to let me have them when the time comes.

Recently, Harold Hardigree, another local descendant, and I were talking about old pictures like those. His interest lay in a snapshot he had of one such portrait he'd seen hanging on a wall of another house. It had been thirty years since I had seen the portraits in Mother's house, and I could not be sure if any of them was related to his. I told Harold I would go through the portraits Mother had, to see if there might be a match.

Mother allowed me to take the backs off the hidden portraits, and immediately I knew they did not match, but my acquaintance with "the nameless photos" was renewed. I found that in viewing these pictures at this later date, I brought with me a more observant eye than I'd had before. Penciled on the backs of both photos were what appeared to be numbers from an estate sale. The number on each portrait started with five and was followed by an item number from an inventory list (5-xxxx). The number 5 would, of course, designate the year. Only a few hundred items separated the two photos in this pair. The backing that held the pictures in one frame was a quarter-inch-thick wooden panel that appeared to be taken from the top of a crate of English mustard. It was brightly colored and carried the coat of arms of England. This seemed odd to me at the time, and even more peculiar was the old, colored sign that had been used as a backing for one of the portraits. It was still in one piece but in poor condition, brittle enough to crumble at the slightest touch. It read "Mahler Bros. January sale of Muslin Underwear, Housekeeping, Cotton and Linens Sixth Ave. Cor. 31 St." I jotted down the information so I could research the findings, and then I tucked the pictures and signs back into the frame as Mother had had them.

Later on that evening, I researched the information online, and in an instant, it all became clear. The information I uncovered that evening helped me understand the time and setting of that dreadful night in May 1905.

[21]Because F. M. Holbrook was a storekeeper and farmer, he made a respectable income for that era. It was obvious to me that the picture backings were remnants of shipping packages that had come from all over the world to his store there on the farm. In this case, one order came from Mahler Brothers in New York City, from which the Holbrooks had ordered cosmetics, perfumes, underwear, and housekeeping goods in 1901. The quarter-inch-thick crate top was from a case of fancy yellow mustard.

The numbers on the back of each portrait obviously represented the estate sale that took place the year of the murders. This sale would have allowed the public and family members a chance to purchase the hundreds of store items made available after the tragedy. The family used proceeds from the estate and store sales to build the Holbrook-Hardigree house in 1908. Because of their use to frame the existing portraits, it is chilling to think that this sign and crate lid also were within feet of the murders on May 9, 1905. As fate would have it, they made their way along, tucked behind the portraits, through the next 109 years. Because of the numbers on the backs of the pictures, it is obvious that Lula, the Holbrooks' only child, purchased her parents' portraits at the estate sale. After all, who else should have owned them? Soon after the sale, these portraits found permanent residency in the new house that Phillip built for Lula in 1908.

---

[21] Ibid.

Papa Ralph was nine years old when he was doubly victimized by the horrific event of his grandparents' murders. Before the first victim of post-traumatic stress disorder was ever diagnosed, Ralph Hardigree had experienced a horror that broke up a loving relationship between him and his grandparents. Ralph was Phillip's eldest child, and because Mother was Ralph's eldest child, Mother recalled, "Daddy would not go out at night alone without me beside him." His condition worsened in 1944. He was shown the oval-framed picture of himself and his beloved grandparents. He took it and flung it across the room. Sadly for him, he remembered very well. Fortunately the picture, frame, and glass were not damaged.

As a general rule, parents would always choose to outlive their children. Oftentimes during our earlier history, this did not happen. The flu pandemic of 1918 would take entire families, beginning with the youngest members. Ralph survived those hardships only to succumb to a more subtle nemesis. He preceded his father in death by seventy-nine days.

The Oconee County sheriff transported Ralph Hardigree Sr. to the Central State Hospital in Milledgeville in 1944. On the trip to the hospital, the sheriff's car broke down, and for a while the men were stranded. Then Ralph asked the sheriff for permission to look under the hood. The sheriff allowed him to do so. After piddling under the hood for a while, Ralph asked the sheriff to start the engine. It turned right over, and they continued on to Milledgeville. The sheriff told the family afterward that he felt it should have been him, not Ralph, staying at the mental hospital.

[22]Frank and Lou Holbrook were buried in the same grave at Johnson Methodist Church on May 11, 1905. Phillip Hardigree was laid to rest on Christmas Day, 1960, next to Lula, who had preceded him by thirty-three years. Papa Ralph was laid to rest at Antioch Christian Church Cemetery on October 7, 1960.

---

[22] Ibid., "Buried in One Grave," May 11, 1905.

The Innocence of Lon J. Aycock

❦ ——◆—— ❧

A t the time of the murders in 1905, there were a number of young black men in the habit of quietly meandering up and down the dirt roads between the country stores. How a white man, Lon J. Aycock, became ensnared with an increasing number of ruthless, younger black men such as Jim Taylor, Sidney Norris, Wiley Durham, Rich Robinson, Lewis Robinson (brother of Rich), and Claude Elder will always be a mystery. Gene Yerby, another black man, was already locked up in the Oconee County jail for stealing a rifle from Mr. Marshall, another nearby storeowner. Many citizens believed that Lon J. Aycock masterminded the conspiracy to rob the Holbrooks. Others believed he was an innocent bystander, in the wrong place at the wrong time, the evening the black gang encountered him and Frank Holbrook at the store.

[23]Several robberies and home invasions had taken place around the community during the several months before the murders, with limited success for the assailants. In some cases, the invasions had ended with the sexual assault of the woman of the house. Already in the Oconee County jail and awaiting sentencing were Joe Patterson, Ed Thrasher, Rick Allen, Will Robertson, and Bob Harris. Some were there for murder; others were there for less than capital crimes.

---

[23] Ibid., "Other Stores Burglarized," May 10, 1905.

Sandy Price was not yet incarcerated, but he became a new resident at the jail after building enough coward's courage to commit an atrocity on Mrs. Dooley of Watkinsville.

Frank Holbrook had previously pressed charges against Claude Elder and the two brothers, Rich and Lewis Robinson, for one of the robberies that occurred at his store. [24]A young black boy who was near John Marshall's house at the time told authorities that he had heard Claude Elder, Rich Robinson, and Lewis Robinson say they were going to kill F. M. Holbrook.

[25]F. M. Holbrook, fifty-eight, and his wife Lou Holbrook, fifty-one, had moved into the community from Banks County and were successfully running a mercantile business. Their store and annex had been under the gang's scrutiny for less-than-honorable reasons. Frank and Lou had left Banks County bound for Oconee County and Mrs. Carrie Hill Marshall's store—which was where the double murder later occurred. [26]Mrs. Marshall was Lou's sister, who had run a millinery at that location for a period of time. Just prior to the Holbrooks' departure from Banks County, a lawsuit was settled in their favor that profited them $900. Some time passed before Frank actually received the cash. [27]News of this cash windfall was hard to keep quiet, especially when Frank was seen depositing the "$900 in a bank in Athens on May 1."

The tension between the Holbrooks and the three black men was obvious. Frank kept his .38-caliber pistol within easy reach. Lou also kept a piece of oak scantling by her bed. It was unlikely the Holbrooks would ever have opened the store for Claude, Rich, or Lewis after hours, since they had recently pressed charges against them. After the murders, some people theorized that Lon Aycock contrived the need for a loan from Frank Holbrook. Others presumed the store was opened when the perpetrator pretended he needed to purchase

---

[24] Ibid., "Negroes had Grudge," May 11, 1905.

[25] Ibid., "The Store was Ransacked," May 11, 1905.

[26] Ibid.

[27] Ibid.

some clothes. [28]Still others believed Lon Aycock needed clothes and money and arranged to borrow $300 from Frank. We will ponder both theories.

[29]Frank returned to Athens sometime after May 1 to draw out $100 for operating capital and $300 for the loan to an unknown person. It appears that Lon Aycock may have been the person for whom the loan was intended. Lon's appointment time with Frank was apparently after normal business hours; Frank had not prepared for bed and was expecting Lon's arrival. Frank let down his guard as he and Lon entered the store annex. The two of them lit enough lanterns and candles to see their way to the suit rack.

On May 9, the night had a thousand eyes—especially at dusk, when a country store like the Holbrooks' lit up at the crossroads. The black gang was obviously in the area, possibly planning another robbery, when the annex along the road lit up. They closed in on their opportunity.

Frank was still wearing his glasses and was showing Lon the clothes on the suit rack when [30]Lewis and Claude Elder rushed into the store. Lewis grasped a flat iron from the sales counter and swung it at Frank Holbrook with deadly intent. He gashed Frank's head open, nearly incapacitating him with one blow. The attack began next to the suit rack, where Frank's glasses were later found on the floor. [31]Blood spatter from that blow and subsequent ones was found on his glasses and the suits on the rack. [32]Claude and Lewis kept their focus on Frank as he began to struggle for his life. Frank yelled out to Lou and ran in the direction of their bedroom.

The scene must have been a blur to Lon as he was immediately outnumbered and ran through the door to safety. He left the scene with nothing he had intended to get. Instinctively, he mounted his horse and left the crime scene at a fast gallop. Once he was a safe

---

[28] Ibid., "Bodies Sadly Mutilated," May 11, 1905.

[29] Ibid.

[30] Ibid.

[31] Ibid.

[32] Ibid.

distance away, he had several things to consider. His poor decisions far outnumbered the one right decision: to notify the law. But he did nothing.

[33]Frank received a continual bashing to the head as the trio fought their way into the bedroom where he kept his pistol. Lou, who had been in bed, picked up the two-by-two piece of oak scantling that she kept there, as Frank frantically staggered toward his firearm. Frank's desperate and final attempt to reach for his pistol was documented by his blood, which was smeared on the wall only inches from where he kept his gun. All in one motion, Claude, who was nearby, saw the object for which Frank was reaching and snatched the pistol away from the dying man. Lewis applied the finishing blows to Frank's mutilated head. Lou struck out at Claude with the scantling as Lewis immediately started to rummage through Frank's pants, searching for the $300 Frank had planned to lend to Lon. [34]As Lou raised the scantling again to defend her mortally wounded husband, [35]Claude Elder grabbed her with both arms and threw her face down, and the sexual assault began.

[36]When they were finished, Lou was shot six times in the back of the head with Frank's pistol, causing the scantling to freeze in her grip. One of the six shots passed through her skull, creating a single exit wound to accompany the six entrance wounds. [37]The brothers found the store's operating cash—about $100—folded in a moneybag inside the pocket of Lou's dress, which was hanging nearby. It is believed the looters were aware that the Holbrooks had more than just the $100; the ransacked condition of the store indicated that the men were searching for more bounty. It would have been impossible to find if Lon had received the loan before the attack occurred. Though only four men were initially incarcerated, the names of three others came out after these four were jailed. The gang was

[33] Ibid., "Three are Arrested for Double Murder," May 11, 1905.

[34] Ibid.

[35] Ibid., "Nine Under Arrest for Murder Near Athens," May 13, 1905.

[36] Ibid., "Bodies Sadly Mutilated," May 11, 1905.

[37] Ibid., "The Store was Ransacked," May 11, 1905.

loosely organized. Claude was the gang leader and the most ruthless. The brothers, Rich and Lewis, were his henchmen and inseparable. Each of them rode bicycles. Jim Taylor, Sidney Norris, and Wiley Durham were on foot and perceived the attack as an invitation to loot immediately after the assault.

The several lanterns that had been lit provided light for the looters. [38]Everything that had value to any of the men was taken, even a new deck of cards. [39]At some point, Taylor and Norris changed the smelly, soiled garb they were seen wearing that night, as they were seen the next day wearing perfectly clean attire. Other members of the gang also disrobed and put on tailor-made items from the Holbrooks' store. The bloody clothes of the perpetrators were likely discarded in the Oconee River or somewhere else along the way to East Athens.

[40]The possibility exists that during the mayhem and the looting, a lantern was knocked over, causing a small fire that prompted the looters to scatter. In the darkness a safe distance away, Lon was still trying to figure out his next move as the looters dispersed. He was aware of the blaze, but he was not aware of Frank and Lou's grave condition. Finally, Lon went back to the aid of the Holbrooks. He dragged their bodies onto the porch, put out the fire, and left the scene. [41]The bodies were found the next morning, side by side, the piece of scantling still in Mrs. Holbrook's hand.

[42]Unknowingly, Claude, Rich, and Lewis had left their individual sets of bicycle tire tracks in the powdery dust at the scene.

The way Lon Aycock chose to handle his predicament was ultimately disastrous. It may have seemed to him that anything he might have done to help the Holbrooks would further implicate him in the crime. He also knew he was the only eyewitness to the crime. He knew he could identify most, if not all, of the six men

---

[38] Ibid., "Three are Arrested for Double Murder," May 11, 1905.
[39] Ibid.
[40] Ibid., "The Store was Ransacked," May 11, 1905.
[41] Ibid.
[42] Ibid.

involved—a fact that would make his life very cheap in the eyes of the murderers and some of the public. But his choice to do nothing made his situation even more precarious. With seven people involved, the innuendos would come easily and the testimony would need careful sorting. Somewhere within the combined knowledge of the seven suspects lay the truth. But getting at that truth would also prove to be very troublesome.

Clearly, the $100 in store operating funds was not all that Claude, Lewis, and Rich had expected to find. No one will ever know if the spoils were divided among the three leaders only or all six men. No one will ever know if Frank withheld the $300 loan until after the purchase of the suits. No one will ever know if the proceeds of the loan went to Lon. There is a real likelihood that, moments before the murders, Lon received the proceeds of that loan. Somewhere in Lon Aycock's last, vehement cry—"You are killing an innocent man!"—lies the answer.

More than likely, at that horrible moment it was every man for himself. Very soon after the first three perpetrators invaded the store, an invitation to loot was apparent, and Jim Taylor, Sydney Norris, and Wiley Durham moved in. These three men had arrived at the scene on foot, but in their haste to leave the scene, they dropped a new deck of cards in a pine thicket a few hundred yards away. That is where the cards were found, with the aid of bloodhounds, the next day. The three may have made their hasty retreat when Lon arrived back at the scene to extinguish the fire or come to the aid of the Holbrooks.

After the seven suspects (including Lon) departed in three or four different directions, only time was needed for each of their inconsistent alibis to surface.

The nighttime song of the crickets, tree frogs, and whippoorwills had been replaced by the songs of the morning birds and the rustling of leaves from a fresh morning breeze. [43]Ten hours had passed since the murders. Slack Anthony, an older black man, walked by the

---

[43] Ibid., May 10, 1905.

store as he had done many times before. But this morning something seemed very strange. Frank and Lou had not opened their store. He called out to Mr. Frank, but there was no answer. He walked to the back of the store where it joined the living quarters. Before he could call out again, he saw the rigid bodies of Frank and Lou on the porch. [44]He hobbled away as quickly as he could, shouting for the Holbrooks' closest neighbor, Adam Smith, who lived a quarter mile away. [45]By noon on May 10, an estimated five to six hundred people had gathered at the scene with mob-like sentiments.

Claude, Rich, and Lewis, the three leaders of the gang, had ridden their bicycles nine miles away to East Athens. By the time the murders were discovered, they were most likely sleeping off their overnight revelry. At eleven in the morning, nine miles southwest of Athens and about three and a half miles south on Greensboro Road near Watkinsville, Jim Taylor and Sydney Norris, who had been on foot the night before, joined the fast-growing crowd of onlookers. This was a critical mistake. Although they had no way of knowing it, Colonel Rose of Athens had been called in with his bloodhounds. The two salivating canines were eager for action as the colonel took them inside the ransacked area of the store. There the dogs obtained a good reference scent and began tugging eagerly at their leashes to follow it.

[46]The hounds lit out on the barefoot trail of Taylor, Norris, and Durham. [47]They had tracked the scent just two hundred yards when they curled and went straight into the crowd where Jim Taylor and Sydney Norris were standing in their clean clothes. The two were immediately detained and taken into the woods where the dogs had gone. There the authorities found the new deck of cards from the store. [48]Taking the suspects into the woods ultimately accomplished two purposes. One was to question them, and the other was to save

[44] Ibid.
[45] Ibid., May 11, 1905.
[46] Ibid.
[47] Ibid.
[48] Ibid.

their lives. The crowd at the murder scene had grown rapidly, and it was becoming more restless by the minute.

In the early evening of May 10, when it was becoming harder to keep the lid on order, rumors of a lynching were first heard. [49]Claude Elder, on his return trip from Athens, was seen pedaling past the murder scene and the impressive crowd of angry citizens. He was immediately deposed, searched, and found to have in his possession Mr. Holbrook's pistol. Afterward he was taken to the jail in Watkinsville for intense questioning. The interrogation yielded three other suspects. At face value, it seemed the officials were unveiling a murder conspiracy. During the questioning, Claude had implicated Lewis Robinson, Rich Robinson, and Lon J. Aycock. The truth about Lon Aycock's involvement was muddied by mixed innuendos from the other suspects.

On May 11, at ten in the morning, the Holbrooks' funeral was held at Johnson Methodist Church, a mile away from the murder scene on Flat Rock Road. Many who were at the scene the day before attended the funeral. Immediately after the funeral, twenty neighbors and friends of the deceased were chosen to be on the citizens' committee to seek out those involved. A citizens' committee in 1905 was equivalent to a homicide investigative unit of today.

[50]The committee members were very diligent in their duties, were fair and somber, and, to their credit, worked rapidly. [51]It seemed to be the committee's intent to jail as many people as it took to get to the truth about the murders. As early as May 12, some of the citizens pleaded with the judge to hold an immediate trial. [52]By May 12, nine individuals who were believed to be involved with the Holbrook murders—three of them were female witnesses—had been jailed. This number did not include those who were already incarcerated. [53]Enough evidence was uncovered by May 25 to arrest

---

[49] Ibid.

[50] Ibid., May 25, 1905.

[51] Ibid.

[52] Ibid., May 11, 1905.

[53] Ibid., May 25, 1905.

and hold four of the seven suspects. [54]Lewis produced the iron used in the murder of Frank. Claude also confessed that it was he, Rich, Lewis, and Lon Aycock who committed the murders. Rich Robinson produced some of the money taken from the deceased. [55]The three black women were held for a short time but were able to produce alibis, and then they, in turn, produced alibis for Taylor, Norris, and Durham.

As terrible as Aycock's predicament had become, jail may have been the safest place for him until trial. Or at least it should have been.

---

[54] Ibid.
[55] Ibid., May 13, 1905.

"Get the Right Ones"

The citizenry of Watkinsville, Georgia, was worked up in a way it had never been before. To many, it seemed that the new jail at the county seat was filling up with young black men who represented a generation bent on having it their own way. Discipline within their ranks was pitifully lacking. Once they became young adults, they found it easier to steal than to work for a living. As a large crowd gathered at the murder scene on May 10, law officials heard Claude Elder's name surface as one possible suspect. Sam Elder, Claude's father and a former slave, respected the rule of law. His statement printed in the *Atlanta Journal* reveals that he obviously had difficulty parenting the twenty-two-year-old. He was heard to say [56]"if his child committed the crime he wanted him killed."

[57]Since all the fatal injuries to the Holbrooks were to the back of the head, their bodies looked reasonably unscathed except for a bruise on Mrs. Holbrook's cheek. There were hundreds of citizens present at Johnson Church at ten o'clock on May 11, when A. A. Sullivan of Watkinsville preached the funeral. [58]Husband and wife were buried in the same grave, one hole deep enough for both caskets.

---

[56] Ibid., "Negroes Had Grudge," May 11, 1905.
[57] Ibid., "Bodies Sadly Mutilated."
[58] Ibid., "Buried in One Grave."

Being Masons, they were buried with full Masonic rites. [59]After the funeral, the citizens' committee was formed.

[60]Between May 11 and May 25, the appointed committee worked day and night, eating only snacks for meals, as they scoured the county and interviewed people to fit together the pieces of the conspiracy puzzle. Jim Taylor, Sydney Norris, and the three women were subsequently (and prematurely) released when their bogus allies cleared them. [61]The committee's two weeks of work implicated Claude Elder, Rich Robinson, Lewis Robinson, and Lon J. Aycock, who remained in jail. Claude Elder confessed that they were the four conspirators, but Lon J. Aycock maintained his innocence. Finally the report was ready.

A large crowd came to the Oconee County courthouse to hear the committee's report. [62]Mr. A. C. Jackson and Representative G. D. Cook gave speeches and thanked the committee for its splendid work. [63]Judge J. C. Johnson then read the report from the courthouse steps, pleading with the crowd for patience as he proceeded with a legal trial.

---

[59] Ibid., "Appeal to Prevent Lynching," May 25, 1905.
[60] Ibid.
[61] Ibid., "State Employs Counsel to Prosecute Murderers," May 28, 1905.
[62] Ibid., "Appeal to Prevent Lynching," May 25, 1905.
[63] Ibid.

1905 Jail

[64]Just two days later, on May 27, the state hired counsel to prosecute the accused murderers. Colonel W. M. Smith was to assist Solicitor General S. J. Tribble. Judge Richard B. Russell Sr. then set the date of the trial for May 31, just three weeks after the date of the crime. After Judge Russell set the date, Rich Robinson began to give up more information, in an obvious attempt to delay matters. [65]Incensed that Jim Taylor and Sydney Norris had been released, he also injected Wiley Durham's name into the quagmire. The committee then considered what they had done by releasing Taylor and Norris earlier, and what they had not done in the case of Wiley Durham, and requested a postponement. The committee obviously felt that all the "right ones" were not incarcerated; [66]at their request, the judge postponed the trial until the July term. The conspiracy obviously ran deeper into the community than he'd realized. The committee thought more information would come forth by July. [67]The postponement further frustrated the public, and "Get the right ones!" would become an echo that would haunt the investigating committee and future generations.

Only over the last century have the majority of American citizens begun to feel reasonably confident in a jury trial to mete out proper justice. Even though trial by jury is not a perfect system, it is the best America has to offer. It is obvious now, in retrospect, that more details about the Holbrooks' murder would have come forth in a jury trial, and those details may have satisfied the curiosity of a justice-seeking public and cleared up the mystery. However, such a trial was not to be. The gossip that had circulated throughout the neighboring counties contained vitriol and vengeance. It would prove to have enough power to put a mob into action and crush the truth—and the structural integrity of the new jail—as though they were eggs.

---

[64] Ibid., "State Employs Counsel to Prosecute Murders," May 28, 1905.

[65] Reed, "Feeling Is Intense Over Mob's Mad Work," June 30, 1905.

[66] "Special Session of Court Postponed at Watkinsville," *Atlanta Journal*, May 31, 1905.

[67] Ibid., May 25, 1905.

The issue of punishment fitting the crime was never addressed in the double-murder conspiracy. With one stroke of vigilante justice, all the jailed prisoners were considered guilty. Lon Aycock's knowledge about the crime would never surface. Lon Aycock had proclaimed the innocence provided to him by the law and trusted that it would be proven in court. But it became painfully obvious that the mob, anxious for revenge, thought Lon had conspired to commit the double murder.

If Lon Aycock was indeed the person for whom the loan of $300 was to be made, might not another scenario also have been a possibility? Clearly, Frank Holbrook and Lon Aycock had agreed that Lon would come by the store after hours, in the early evening. What if he'd simply wanted to secure the loan and buy some clothes? Was the loan made to Lon just before Frank was attacked and the sale of the suit was interrupted? Having $300 in Lon's possession would have looked very incriminating. Could Claude, Rich, and Lewis have overheard information about the loan arrangements, followed Lon's every move, and taken the $300 from Lon just moments before he escaped?

The Straw That Broke the Camel's Back

ംരൂ ——◉—— ഉ

The new jail behind the Oconee County courthouse had just been completed. By June 29, 1905, it held ten individuals, the charges against them ranging from gambling and robbery to murder. Lon Aycock was the only white prisoner. When the trial for the double murder of F. M. and Lou Holbrook was postponed until July, the public may have wondered how many cells were in the jail. Some of the inmates there had already been tried and were awaiting execution. After the committee's investigation, four more were arrested and sent to jail to await trial. [68]What seemed best for Oconee County was to follow the due process of the law. The county settled in to wait for the additional evidence and the July court trial.

In those days, the less dangerous inmates, charged with lesser offenses, were kept on one side of the jail, the "misdemeanor side." The more violent inmates, charged with or convicted of serious offenses, were held on the other side. [69]Only one prisoner was incarcerated on the misdemeanor side, a gambler named Ed Thrasher. Joe Patterson also was being held at the jail for pointing a pistol at Albert Ward, a member of the committee, during the course of the investigation. This may have been the least serious charge among the inmates

---

[68] Reed, "Mob Undoes Work," June 30, 1905.
[69] Wilkes.

on the other side. Rich Allen was there awaiting execution for the murder of Will Robertson; another black man, Bob Harris, was awaiting trial for shooting two other black men near Bishop, Georgia; and Gene Yerby was charged with stealing a rifle from Mr. Marshall. As of May 25, Lon J. Aycock was the only white man in the jail. Lewis Robinson, Rich Robinson, and Claude Elder were also incarcerated there for the double-murder conspiracy. The jail was like a pot that was full to the brim. It was about to boil over as the heat intensified.

As justly wrought up as Oconee County was, neighboring counties were even more so. In Banks County, relatives and neighbors of the Holbrooks had thought highly of Frank, Lou, and their only daughter, Lula. They had been a benevolent Masonic family, and this atrocity was a disgrace. The question might be asked, Was there ever a time that the wheels of justice turned too slowly? It certainly seemed that, in this particular era of the twentieth century, this might have been the case. It favored some of the incarcerated but hastened the execution of others. If you were innocent and that fact could be proven when trial came, the system worked against you, because the vigilantes were hot. If more guilty parties were still roaming the dirt roads of Oconee County, time was on their side. It became obvious that vigilantes had been meeting with quiet resolve in the shadows of the surrounding counties, waiting for orders from their secret leaders.

At this early time in America's legal history, fear could still result in mob rule. [70]The general belief among the law-abiding majority in the region, and those few who would take the law into their own hands, was that their homes and lives were being threatened by the recent wave of violence.

Wyatt Earp and Bat Masterson, who were enjoying retirement, were of this same generation and had helped quell civil unrest in the new western towns of Wichita, Kansas, Dodge City, Kansas, and Tombstone, Arizona. Only twenty-five years separated those events and the Holbrook murders. By today's standards, the Earp brothers, and Doc Holliday too, would have been guilty of some

---

[70] Reed, "The Assault Brand," June 30, 1905.

violations of legal protocol. Today, a highly trained detective team would have gathered all the evidence within a forty-eight-hour period, instead of the twenty neighbors and friends who formed the citizens' investigating committee in 1905.

Ironically, enough time was granted for the citizens' committee to "get the right ones" for the cause of justice. But this same period of time was also used by the vigilantes to plan and execute a lynching. The term *lynching* evokes a mental picture of a rope and a tree limb. Though often those might have been the handiest tools with which to effect an execution, *lynching*, by its truest definition, means putting someone to death by mob action without due process of the law.

The scales of justice were about to be tipped. Who could have known what was in the mind of Sandy Price? Maybe he thought himself more cunning than his peers awaiting trial and execution. And his plan might have been foolproof if he could have kept it secret, and if there were no witnesses to his lusty pursuits. But he did not expect the fight Mrs. Dooley would give him on June 22, 1905, just outside the town of Watkinsville.

[71]Mrs. Weldon Dooley was alone in her home during the afternoon of June 22 when Sandy Price happened upon her and attempted to sexually assault her. She struggled free of her assailant, and with all the commotion that ensued, Price fled. [72]Immediately after the incident, neighbors ran Price down, firing several shots after him. He was neither wounded nor harmed, as cooler heads prevailed in the matter, and he was carried to jail for safekeeping. However, when news of Sandy Price's assault on Mrs. Dooley reached the neighboring counties, those secret leaders had only to give the order. A volatile plan had been in the works since the postponement of the double-murder trial, and this new assault lit the fuse. It is only a guess, but I'd say if there were a thousand citizens willing to wait for a jury verdict, there were a thousand more ready for a more immediate conclusion. [73]Out of this polarizing split, inevitably, there would come

---

[71] Reed, "What Caused the Lynching?," June 30, 1905.
[72] Ibid.
[73] Ibid.

an informer who would bring a rumor that had been on the wind for nearly two months. On June 28, A. N. Bostwick came to Watkinsville from Morgan County with news of a planned lynching. The mob entered Watkinsville the next day.

To say that Sheriff Overby knew any of the details of the lynching would not do justice to the man or the office of sheriff. [74]The lynching was so precisely planned that the organizers had thought to schedule it for Overby's day off; he would be on his farm and would not be back in Watkinsville until the next day.

At an undisclosed location outside Watkinsville, the mob met precisely at midnight on June 29, 1905. [75]It is presumed they came with enough saddle horses and buggies to accommodate approximately one hundred riders. [76]They masked their faces and then proceeded to the house of Marshall L. H. Aiken, who held the key to the jail. [77]Only one man spoke for the mob, and his voice and face were unrecognizable. Aiken would not give up the key, so the mob grabbed him by the neck and took him at gunpoint to the jail. [78]The leader of the mob then directed the man on his right to get the blacksmith, though his services would not be needed when they reached the jail.

[79]It was about one in the morning when A. W. Ashford overheard the mob at Akien's home and rushed to get dressed. [80]By the time he could catch up with the crowd, they were already near the courthouse. There he was stopped by one of the masked vigilantes and asked what his intent was. Then the mob continued in the direction of the new jail, which was directly behind the courthouse. Ashford later reported that he didn't recognize the man or his voice. [81]Ashford scanned the masked crowd and determined they were not from Oconee County.

---

[74] Ibid., June 29, 1905.
[75] Ibid., "The Mob Worked Silently."
[76] Ibid., "Mob Rode Silently Into Town."
[77] Ibid.
[78] Wilkes.
[79] Reed, "Mob Rode Silently into Town."
[80] Ibid.
[81] Ibid.

[82]From his spot in the crowd, Mr. Ashford saw Marshall Akien open the outside doors of the jail. As Mr. Ashford made his way through the mob to the front of the building, he started pleading to the crowd to spare the life of Lon J. Aycock because there was no evidence to convict him. [83]But the leader of the mob obviously knew him, saying, "It is no use talking, Mr. Ashford, they are determined."

[84]Jailer Crow was awakened by the noise at the door of the jail building. As he approached it, the mob pushed in and overwhelmed him. At first he refused to give up the cell keys, but soon he realized that there was no use resisting, for the men could accomplish their mission without opening the cell doors.

---

[82] Ibid., "Pleaded for Aycock."

[83] Ibid.

[84] Ibid., "Jailer Crow's Version of Watkinsville Tragedy," June 29, 1905.

The Actions of the Mob

ଔୠ ——⊶◉⊷—— ୠଔ

[85] Each member of the mob had been given a task and went about it with quiet determination. Except for the rattle of the keys and the clanking of iron, nothing else could be heard from the mob. [86]First they tied the hands of the accused behind their backs and methodically placed a rope around each man's neck. This was a means of securing them for temporary transport to the back of the jail. Behind the jail stood three tall, wooden posts that held up the hog wire of a hog pen. The broken board at the top of the wire was unable to keep it from sagging. They tied the men's heads high on the three tall posts in standing position. One of the prisoners started pleading, giving up additional information. [87]Rich Robinson implicated others, and Lon Aycock proclaimed his innocence, declaring, "You're killing an innocent man!" But the rest were numb. Each post temporarily secured three prisoners until the speedy execution was ordered.

[88]It was a dark night in every sense of the word. Only two lanterns offered perspective on the distance for accurate firing; they were placed on either side of the group to light up the condemned. The

---

[85] Reed, "Feeling Intense over Mob's Mad Work," June 30, 1905.
[86] Wilkes.
[87] Reed, "Aycock Believed Innocent," June 30, 1905.
[88] Ibid, "The Final Scene."

mob formed a tight semicircle around the nine men. [89]The leader of the mob then stepped back only a few feet and fired. On that signal, the night lit up like midday as the first two ranks also fired. The muzzle flash from black powder pistols, shotguns, and repeating rifles was later described as a single ebb and flow that lasted only a few seconds.

[90]It is presumed the men in the front knelt and fired first. The second group fired over their shoulders, in Civil War fashion. Likewise, the second rank then knelt as the third and final volley lit up the night. A building that lay beyond, serving as one side of the hog pen, was also the backstop for the firing squad. No time was wasted. Three volleys were planned, but the individual sound of each volley was indistinguishable. Only those men with repeating weapons continued to fire until a smokescreen of black powder covered the targets. [91]In less than a minute after the first shot was fired, the mob had scattered into the darkness, leaping into their saddles and buggies. Unlike the way they came, they dispersed in all different directions. None went toward Athens.

The vigilantes made every effort to succeed in their mission, but two attributes of the Almighty, justice and mercy, played out in those fleeting moments. [92]Back at the jail, the gambler Ed Thrasher's prayer for mercy had been answered, as he hid under his bed when vengeance came to call. [93]Outside, when the signal to fire was given, several rounds caused Joe Patterson's legs to give way, and his head slipped through the noose as he fell unconscious to the ground beneath his slain comrades. Mercy was granted him as well.

It was almost two in the morning on June 29, 1905, in Watkinsville, Georgia. The sound of galloping saddle horses and the rattle of moving buggy tack had subsided. (The vigilantes had used no slow-moving mules and wagons for their mission.) Shortly after

---

[89] Wilkes.

[90] Reed, "The Bodies Were Riddled," June 30, 1905.

[91] Ibid.

[92] Wilkes.

[93] Ibid.

the lynching, an eerie calm had fallen, and now only four citizens remained on the streets of this small southern town in Georgia. Those four—Marshall L. H. Aiken; Mr. A. W. Ashford; the jailer, Crow; and the blacksmith—stood in trembling shock. What had just occurred was, at the time, one of the worst miscarriages of justice in American history. It did not have the flare and sensational quality of the Gunfight at the O.K. Corral, but nevertheless, it was an unlawful attempt to deter an outbreak of crime that seemed to require drastic measures.

[94]The bodies of the executed lay as they had fallen long after the sun rose, rendering a grisly scene for the waking public. The citizens picked up empty shell casings, which contaminated any effort to identify the mobsters. Dr. L. W. Hodges examined the bodies when daylight came. [95]He found that Joe Patterson was still breathing, with only a grazed head wound and two flesh wounds. Rich Robinson had been fatally shot in the mouth. [96]In addition to Aycock's body being riddled with bullet holes, the hole in his chest, where his heart had been, was as big as a man's fist. Incredibly, some people had considered him the guiltiest of them all. The end result of the execution was eight dead.

[97]The executioners' marksmanship, even in the darkness, was incredible, and the number and location of each prisoner's wounds told a story in itself. Wounds to the mouth and heart gave some indication of the perception of guilt or innocence that the firing squad had for the executed. The taller ones still stood, their ghastly faces staring upward, and the shorter ones leaned against them, all in a mortal heap.

In 1983, at a Hardigree reunion, its organizers made the Holbrooks' double murders the theme for that year. Our relatives were asked to bring anything that was related to the case. At the reunion, my uncle Ralph was presented the Holbrook pistol, a .38

---

[94] Ibid.

[95] Ibid.

[96] Ibid.

[97] Ibid.

revolver, from a great-uncle. He later passed it on to one of his sons, Scott Hardigree. But the most gripping of all the memorabilia was a picture of the slain prisoners.

[98]On May 25, 1905, when the investigating report was read to the citizens of Oconee County, Judge Johnson had made a direct appeal to the public, pleading with the citizens to allow the due process of law to take its course, and reminding them that the eyes of the state—and the world—were watching. The day after the lynching, June 30, the Georgia House of Representatives passed a resolution condemning the action of the mob. While the legislators used strong language to describe the action, in the end they let it be known they were being forced to condemn the action of the mob.

---

[98] "Appeal to Prevent Lynching," *Atlanta Journal,* May 25, 1905.

The Executed

Phillip Hardigree's Lineage

In early American culture, large families were normal. With the difficulties of childbearing came the attrition of the female body, which often meant that a mother would pass on, leaving eight to ten children of various ages. Then, in most cases, the man would remarry out of necessity and start a second family within the same household. This large aggregate of children, sometimes numbering as many as twenty or more, meant the household needed strict order and a chain of command. With so many children to feed and educate, it also meant the parents taught each member certain responsibilities that fit his or her age and capability. It often meant the eldest child had early on been trained in every area of family responsibility. It was incumbent upon that child, male or female, to aid the parents in directing the younger siblings in the accomplishment of their family chores. This freed the mother and father to focus on matters above and beyond the day-to-day necessities of food, shelter, and clothing. The parents would spend this time seeking out a better life for the family.

As a baby boomer and also the last of a family of six, it has been my observation that my mother and father placed more responsibility on my eldest brother than on the rest of us siblings. As each of us grew into different phases of our lives, it was plain to see that our parents, too, had been nurtured in this vestige of early-American culture. I was struck by the fact that my father was the eldest in his family; my mother the eldest in hers; my mother's father, Ralph, the eldest in Phillip's family; and Phillip the eldest in his. Certainly with this many elder siblings from each generation parenting the next, there had to be a uniquely positive effect on the family structure.

The Elder-Hardigree book by Ernest Elder is a treasure trove of information on the earliest known records for surnames that are prominent in this area of northeastern Georgia. It notes that Jonathan Hardigree was born in Maryland in 1775 as one of four children to an undocumented Hardigree family. Jonathan died in Coweta County, Georgia, between the years 1860 and 1870. The small number of children in his immediate family may indicate that their parents died young, but this is only a supposition. Jonathan had an older sister named Eleanor; a younger sister, Mary; and a baby brother, William. To my knowledge, these are the earliest Hardigrees in America, though a more thorough search of the Maryland records could reveal more.

We can document Jonathan in Caswell County, North Carolina, where he married Martha "Patsy" Cameron in 1797. This bond produced six sons and two daughters by the year 1814. With John's second wife, Mary "Polly" Giles, a reversal occurred: she bore seven daughters and two sons. It is apparent that there were many Hardigree descendants from Jonathan alone. The migration and settlement of these siblings were in accordance with the land Jonathan acquired. Two sons from his first marriage, Pleasant and Joel, settled in Clarke County, Georgia, around 1843. Some years later, their father moved on to Coweta County.

[99]By all accounts, Jonathan Hardigree was a land speculator. He had significant holdings in Clarke County and was included in the early membership of men at the Christian Church at Old Republican. In 1843, at the age of sixty-seven, he withdrew from the Christian Church membership and moved on, leaving his land

---

[99] Lavender, 293.

holdings in Clarke County (now Oconee County) to his two sons, Pleasant and Joel, who continued to live there.

For reasons unknown, from this early time forward, the descendants from these two brothers were considered two different sets of Hardigrees. My father told me that the Hardigrees who descended from Pleasant were unrelated to those who descended from Joel. I found this difficult to believe, and my research revealed their kinship. It would be very interesting to know what precedent created such a wall between two full-blooded brothers in the middle of the nineteenth century. However, the family reunions are still held separately, even today, at the same church. I sincerely doubt anyone in the family even knows why. Both brothers lived and died in what is now Oconee County. It is believed that Pleasant is buried in an old family cemetery off Carruth Road, while Joel is in a family cemetery off Jerusalem Road. The graves are not even a mile apart. The following Rudyard Kipling poem may best explain their relationship:

[100]Oh, East is East and West is West and never the twain shall meet,
Till Earth and Sky stand presently at God's great Judgment seat.
But there is neither East nor West, Border, nor Breed nor Birth,
When two strong men stand face to face though they come
    from the ends of the earth.

In 1842, the earliest year for which the church membership was recorded, the male leaders of the Antioch Christian Church were listed by number, starting with David Elder Sr. (1760–1863), Edmond Elder (1788–1875), Samuel Blakely (1786–1868), Jonathan Hardigree (1775–1865), David Willoughby (1790–1853), and so forth. There were just as many women in a separate numerical listing. The total membership in 1842 was approximately ninety men and women.

Phillip's grandfather, Joel, had a large family of eleven, in which the traditional concept of birthright and responsibilities would have

---

[100] Rudyard Kipling, *The Ballad of East and West* (1889), excerpted, Bartleby.com, http://www.bartleby.com/246/1129.html (accessed August 14, 2014), par. 1.

been observed. A significant number of Phillip's aunts and uncles on the Hardigree side of the family died before he was born and thus would have had no influence on his life at all. However, Phillip's uncle Samuel David Hardigree (October 24, 1836–January 21, 1917) and his uncle James Phillip Hardigree (June 7, 1857–May 1, 1915), for whom he was named, could have helped nurture into maturity the fatherless thirteen-year-old boy, the eldest child of five. I can only imagine the dominant influence his mother, Fannie Thomas (1849–1921), would have had upon Phillip after his father's death in 1886. A tremendous responsibility had been placed on the shoulders of the eldest child of the family.

Though the traditional American family structure has come under attack in recent decades, with the increased divorce rate, same-sex marriages, and two-income households, it has been my observation—and I believe history will prove—that the strength of America is directly proportional to the strength of its traditional families.

Phillip and Lula

A Short Biography of Phillip Hardigree

ᴄᴱᏕ ──── ᏸᴱᴾ

J ames Phillip Hardigree was born to General Lazarus Hardigree
and Francis (Fannie) A. Thomas on September 5, 1873. The effects
of losing a father at age thirteen is hard to measure, but surely it had
some bearing on Phillip's and his family's life in the years to come.
Those who knew him characterized Phillip as an eccentric. Being
eccentric is not necessarily a bad thing, but I suppose that in some
cases it could be. Some of our finest citizens (many inventors, for
example) were eccentrics. Whether Phillip intended to be the way
he was, or whether he simply was a product of his circumstances, we
may never know.

Phillip was most likely working in Banks County, Georgia, when
at age nineteen he married seventeen-year-old Emma Lula Holbrook
on December 20, 1894. He would support his family by farming
and judging timber. My grandfather, Ralph, was born to them on
September 23, 1895.

Four years later in Banks County, a photographer was provided
an opportunity to photograph three generations of the Holbrooks
at their homeplace there. That is the photograph that hangs over
my mother's bed in an oval, beveled-glass picture frame. It shows
my grandpa, Ralph, age four; his mother, Emma Lula Holbrook
Hardigree, age twenty-one; and her parents, Francis M. Holbrook,

age fifty-three, and Lou Hill Holbrook, age forty-seven. The year would have been 1899, not long before Francis and Lou would purchase a forty-one-acre farm at the location of the only home I have ever known. Lou's sister had run a millinery store in the same house and store annex on this forty-one-acre tract. Phillip's family and many of his friends also lived in the same area of Oconee County.

Sometime around 1900 in Banks County, Francis (Frank) learned he would receive a settlement of $900. This cash windfall could have encouraged him and Lou to purchase the farm in the Astondale estate area of Oconee County.

Four other children were born to Phillip and Lula between 1899 and 1908. It is believed that the two eldest children were born in Banks County, and the others were born after the family's move to Oconee County. Ralph was the eldest. Then came my great-aunt Lurah Hardigree, born on February 13, 1899; great-uncle Lester Francis Hardigree on February 16, 1902; great-aunt Trudie Hardigree on October 6, 1903; and great-aunt Ebbie Elgie Hardigree on July 26, 1908. Though all of the above are now deceased, my great-aunts and -uncles were as dear to my immediate family as my closer relatives.

Phillip and Lula settled in the Astondale estate area south of Watkinsville in 1903, living in several different locations within that community over the next fifty-seven years. Little is known about the two-thousand-acre Astondale estate except that it was dissolved by numerous land purchases, such as the one that F. M. Holbrook made in 1901. However, the children living in the community were educated at the Astondale School during the first two decades of the twentieth century. The school burned in 1922, after Grandpa Ralph and my great-aunts and -uncles had finished school there. For many years, a lone oak tree remained near where the school burned, and then the tree, too, had a fiery demise fifteen or twenty years ago, when it was struck by lightning. Now all that remains to remind us of this vast Astondale estate is Astondale Road, which connects the school end of Highway 15, where my mother lives now, and Bishop, Georgia. Mother has commented many times that her Grandma

Lula boarded teachers in the new home that Phillip built for them after the deaths of her parents in 1908.

Lula and Phillip first lived in the Vandiver house off Highway 15 in 1903; they later purchased it. The house was located about a half mile east of Frank and Lou's forty-one acres, and it was where they were living when the double murder of Frank and Lou Holbrook occurred in 1905. This event was deeply disturbing not only to Lula, but to Ralph, the Holbrook's eldest grandchild, who was only nine years old. Mother believes that her father never put the trauma of this event out of his mind. It seems that Phillip tried to put some distance between Ralph and Lula and the area of the murders. He moved the family a mile east, to the Howard Ward place on Oliver Bridge Road. He later purchased this house and farm—a move that became a business pattern. Except for their marriage in Banks County and the Moultrie excursion, the Howard Ward home is about as far from the Astondale vicinity as Phillip and Lula ever lived.

As family folklore has plucked my heartstrings, so did the stories from the decades before mother's birth stick in her fascinated memory. The stories were told over and over so many times that it almost seemed to Mother that she had actually lived those years leading up to the Moultrie trip.

Thus far, Phillip's ability to purchase the farms that he worked lay in his skill at judging timber and the reciprocal nature of selling the trees and buying the land. With the coming Great Depression, when cash would be limited, this business practice would work very well for him in Oconee County. But what he really needed was a grubstake that would catapult him toward his fortune.

In 1916, Phillip pooled his resources and purchased a five-hundred-acre cotton farm in Moultrie, Georgia. By 1917, with the exception of Aunt Ebbie, all of Phillip's children had finished school at Astondale, and so Phillip seized the opportunity to farm cotton in Moultrie. Before leaving for Moultrie, Ralph married my grandmother, Cleo Wilkes, and approximately two months later she became pregnant with my mother, Ruby Neal. The entire family, including Cleo, moved into a large house in Moultrie, near the fields where they worked using eighteen mules.

In 1974, I was fortunate enough to be with them on a return trip to the area to see how that single five-hundred-acre tract of land would appear. Since Mother was only two years old in 1920, she needed help from her Aunt Ebbie to find her birthplace. Though it was near the city limits of Moultrie, it was still on the poor side of town. It was a rather drab setting for modern times, located by the same railroad tracks that were there in 1918. Aunt Ebbie used the railroad tracks as a landmark to precisely pinpoint the address.

The large house they had all lived in was dilapidated, and the nearby barn was likewise in shambles, a dumb witness to the life that abounded there long ago. There were a few trees scattered about, and the land was flat and appeared sparsely populated. Apparently it was considered an even more remote area than it has been in earlier years, when cotton was king (now peanuts rule). Today, access to Moultrie is aided by Interstate 75, and the city is best known as the setting for North America's Premiere Farm Show, which features a host of farming exhibitions, livestock competitions, and grand food events.

During the two seasons they lived in Moultrie, Phillip netted a $20,000 profit farming cotton. Ruby Neal Hardigree was born there on March 31, 1918. Phillip and Lula's second grandchild came into the world as a blue and still baby, and later her aunts and uncles would repeatedly describe the joyous and tearful celebration that erupted when she caught her first breath. They told the stories over and over about how they would rush from the fields when the dinner bell rang—not to eat, but to hold Ruby Neal. In the scriptures it is written to "honor thy father and mother that you may live long on the earth." In some part, if not all, I believe that is why my mother is still in good health and breathing just fine in 2014.

Phillip's daughter Lurah married Doc Hardigree, and Geneva Hardigree was born to them, giving Phillip and Lula their first grandchild. Though Geneva Hardigree was born to Lurah two months before my mother's birth, she was in Watkinsville and Ruby Neal was in Moultrie.

Mother still chuckles at a story from that time, which has survived for ninety-six years: that Phillip would hold her at lunchtime, and her aunts and uncles observed her banging him on the head with a hairbrush.

The first home that Ralph and Cleo had to themselves in Oconee County was the same Vandiver farmhouse that Phillip had bought before building his and Lula's large white house in 1908. It sat at the end of a long driveway that accessed the Vandiver land from Greensboro Road. Over one hundred acres of the Vandiver place stretched from the end of this driveway over to what is now Kirkland Road. It was 1919, and Mother was two years old, when she, Ralph, and Cleo moved into the Vandiver house after returning from Moultrie.

The $20,000 grubstake Phillip had obtained in Moultrie allowed him to widen his timber and land speculations to the surrounding areas of Oconee County. Now, having ready cash, he was a walking bank at a time when cash was nearly extinct. How true the story is, no one knows, but it has been said that at one time or another during his lifetime, Phillip Hardigree held the deed to every property in the southern half of Oconee County. His holdings accumulated, but he never intended to keep all the property for which he held the deeds. To him the land was just a commodity.

Page 8, The Oconee Enterprise, Thursday, August 29, 1974

ASTONDALE SCHOOL - GREENSBORO Road. 1911 - Burned in 1922

1st row [l-r] sitting: Sue Bee Elder, Trudie Hardigree, Mary Downs, Inez Marshall, Violet Smith, Ruby and Roseanell Leachman, Clyde Elder, Lamar Elder, Carl Payne, Ernest Elder.

2nd row [L-R] standing: Lillian Miller, Otis Hardigree, Jimmy Thomas, Harold Elder, Doris Marshall, Omar McCree, Tom Mcree, Will Henry Marshall, Hanson Smith, Hoke Smith, Carlton Downs, Frank Elder.

3rd row: Warner Edge, Teacher, Lester Hardigree, Clovis Elder, Marvin Thomas, Walter Miller, Nathern Elder, Marvin Elder, Waymon Thomas.

4th row: Katie Mae Lile, Ann Mae Elder, Lila Mathis, Lois Hardigree, Lura Hardigree, Webb Hardigree, Ralph Hardigree, and Collie Mathis. Submitted by: Mrs. Gwen E. Hansford and Marvin T. Elder.

Astondale School circa 1920

When Astondale School burned in 1922, Mother began attending school in Watkinsville. Today the red-brick building still stands as an office building. Through my adolescence, this was an elementary school for grades one through three. In Mother's day it was for grades one through eleven. Today in Oconee County, we have a separate elementary school for grades one through four, an intermediate school for grades five and six, a junior high for seven and eight, and two high schools, North Oconee High School and Oconee County High, with size designations of AAAA. (Larger than A, AA, and AAA. AAAA is the largest classification.)

In those days before carpooling and school buses, the only way to get to and from school was by horse and buggy. The old Greensboro Road ran behind what is today the Shell station at the city limits of Watkinsville. The area closest to where the Shell station is today was too swampy for horse-and-buggy travel, so Greensboro Road was formed a quarter mile east and up the grade by fifteen decades of this mode of travel.

In the spring of 1924, Erskine Marshall, Catherine Marshall, and Ruby Neal loaded into a buggy and made their way to school. (The only place for Ruby Neal to sit was on the buggy floor.) The creek was swollen where they usually crossed, and as the buggy approached this swollen area, the horse balked. When Erskine used his buggy whip, the horse kicked Ruby Neal in the head. She was knocked unconscious for a while, and the concussion kept her out of school for a number of weeks.

After the accident, Ralph contrived a better way to transport Ruby Neal to school. He paid Mr. Lloyd Downs two dollars a week to drop her off at school in Watkinsville. Soon, carpooling with alternate drivers became the primary means of transporting children to school. In 1932, Bill Murray started a school bus route, and eighty-two years later, Oconee County has a whole fleet of buses that go in all different directions.

In 1926, Mother's Aunt Molly and Uncle Lester Hardigree were in charge of the youth program at Antioch Christian Church. Even today, Mother can still recite the poem that was her part in the Christmas play eighty-eight years ago:

> *I told my brother Jim today*
> *He must quit pulling the kittens' tails*
> *Or Santa wouldn't come our way.*
> *Santa might surely forget*
> *To come on Christmas Eve*
> *And not a single little toy*
> *For bad boys would he leave.*
> *For Jim he hurts the kittens*
> *And steals the pies and cakes*
> *And gets in Mama's cupboard,*
> *And all the jam he takes!*
> *Now I have been just as good as gold,*
> *And kept my dresses just as clean,*
> *And minded Mama when she said*
> *Not to be heard but seen.*
> *I dusted the chairs and swept the floors,*
> *And they look just as slick!*
> *I know Santa will bring me toys,*
> *But Jim will get a stick!*

Mother joined Antioch Christian Church the next year and was baptized in the cold spring waters of its first baptismal pool, on the Lowe-Morton farm adjacent to the church.

In 1928, Ruby Neal was ten, and Ralph and Cleo were still living in the Vandiver house off Greensboro and Kirkland Roads. The house was tucked into the woods more than a quarter mile from Greensboro Road. More than one hundred farming acres connected it to Kirkland Road. At that time, all the roads south of Watkinsville were dirt. Greensboro Road was the main artery into Greene County from Oconee County. Many secondary roads and driveways still intersect this route over its entire length. Mother would ride her horse when she wasn't in school, but she walked the distance from the house to the main road on school days. Ruby Neal was not a small girl, and neither was she large, but "above-average height and size" might well describe her. At age ninety-six, she carries 165 pounds very well. Daily exercise and farm chores made Ruby Neal a very strong adolescent girl. That strength was instrumental in saving her life one fateful day, when Ralph was returning from the railroad depot in Watkinsville.

Ralph was driving a young team of mules pulling a wagonload of fertilizer. When he saw Ruby Neal at the intersection of their driveway and Greensboro Road, he shouted out for her to stand clear of the wagon, fearing she might spook the inexperienced team of mules. Mother ignored his warning and jumped onto the load of fertilizer, but soon she discovered that she had no grip. She slid from the hard, slick sacks and fell in front of the rear wagon wheel. She was literally run over by a wagonload of fertilizer. She broke several lower ribs, but everyone was very thankful she was alive. Today, when doctors see the scars from that long-ago accident, they ask if she was in an automobile wreck. "Not exactly, " she replies. "I was run over by a mule-team wagonload of fertilizer."

Mother was given a horse for multiple purposes. One was to bust middles in the field, and the other was for transportation. At an early age, Mother would ride her horse between their house and the Marshalls' house on the main road where the accident occurred. In those days, before Vernon Downs acquired the land and house where the Marshalls lived, Will Henry and Doris Marshall would, on occasion, help Mother onto the horse's back because of the sheer size difference between a ten-year-old girl and a fifteen-hand horse.

Mother said the horse was stubborn about "get up" when the plow was hooked to it. Acting on a recommendation from a neighbor, Papa Ralph wired a magneto to the trace chains to shock the horse when it would not go. Mother would crank the magneto, and the horse would plow lively for a while and then stop. Then Mother would crank it again. She said the horse finally became broke of balking, and it would plow the row middles with a single "Get up!" command.

Phillip's youngest daughter, Ebbie, married Luther Suttles on April 26, 1928. Ruby Neal was a bright girl of ten years old when her Grandma Lula died of a dental infection exactly one month later. Mother has described many times how Lula lay in state in Mother's present bedroom on May 26, 1928. Phillip was fifty-six by then, and most of his children were out of the nest. He had also attained considerable wealth. The combination of these circumstances did not help his personal case of the "middle-age crazies." It seemed to the family that his marital vows "till death do us part" applied to the rest of the family as well. It was Lula's land and Lula's house. She chose to leave each member of the family with an equal part interest. Later, Ruby Neal's Aunt Trudie bought up each of the children's parts so she would have controlling interest and not Phillip. She then was able to assist our family in moving onto the property.

Aunt Ebbie was the last of his children to fly the nest after Lula's death, leaving a rich, lonely man in a big, lonely house. It was Phillip's life to live, but the way he approached his romances seemed reckless and lacking forethought. Then again, he may not have even cared. This "throw caution to the wind" attitude landed him in some hot water, especially with his immediate family members, who at this point were feeling abandoned. During this time of the Great Depression, Phillip Hardigree was ranked among the wealthiest men in the county, if not the state. Having cash, especially when the majority of Americans had none, allowed him to be as eccentric as he wanted to be. He bought up vast amounts of property, one being the Early Thomas cotton gin and surrounding land. Much to the chagrin of Phillip's immediate family, he began to court and later married Early Thomas's widow, Edna Thomas.

Ruby Neal's name was soon to become Sister, as her younger siblings, Agnes, Thomas, Eugene, and Ralph Jr., joined the family. All her brothers are now deceased, leaving Mother and Agnes as the only surviving children. Agnes still refers to Mother as Sister, reminding me of the countless times I have heard her siblings affectionately poke fun at her and address her in that manner. The siblings didn't speak the name as a mere acknowledgment of their relationship, but with an overtone of respect for her as the eldest.

Stocks of Hay and Hands of Fodder

"I was raised to be a boy," Mother often says, but her grace and beauty make that a ludicrous statement. When asked the secret of her longevity, she gives this short response: "Hard work." These two remarks reflect the truism that during the Great Depression, male and female worked side by side, often with little distinction. Another assumption may be derived from the fact that if Ralph and Cleo's first child had been a boy, they would have named him Neal. Because she was a girl, she was named Ruby, thus Ruby Neal.

Following in his father's footsteps, Ralph purchased a 180-acre farm on Elder Mill Road. The land had sufficient timber to make it affordable. Soon one of Mother's primary jobs was milking the cow before school. She also fed and penned the milk cow in the evening, keeping her separate from her calf until the next morning's milking was over. Since a cow's udder has four quarters, one was left for the calf to nurse. Within a year this calf would provide fresh and tender beef for the family.

Soon after Ralph's family moved to Elder Mill Road, and still before the time of school buses, a local carpool was developed to transport the community kids to Watkinsville. This arrangement lasted for a couple of years, until the school bus era began in the mid-1930s. Ralph's house was located approximately three quarters of a mile from Elder's Covered Bridge. The covered bridge was well built and more than a hundred feet long. It covered a vast expanse over the shoals of Rose Creek and its noisy water flow. The children's destination each morning was through the covered bridge and up the other side of the hill to Shannon Elder's house, where they met with others in the carpool. As Ruby Neal walked to school with the other children, many notorious and spooky tales about the covered bridge were told. Doc and Frances Elder had lived in the first house up the hill from the bridge and on the left. When they were murdered, their bodies were thrown under Elder's Covered Bridge. Mother and the children would run as fast as they could through the shadows of the bridge to reach the other side. It takes little imagination to hear the rapid patter of the children's shoeless feet echoing in the covered bridge.

In 2014, when it is my turn to sit with Mother from early evening until nine o'clock in the morning, she often recalls many of the old-fashioned ways she and Dad passed along to us boys. She likes to tell of the short but memorable episodes that were closely tied to her farm chores.

When Mother was twelve, she and Agnes both helped their mother, Cleo, with the household chores. However, before they walked the mile to Shannon Elder's house, Mother had certain morning chores to do. Using two earthen churns, she would mix most of the fresh milk with a cup of clabber from the previous day's milking. She would then churn the clabbered milk from the previous day into butter—the clabber sped up the process—leaving a byproduct of buttermilk needed for drinking, cooking, and feeding the hogs. When Mother was not in school, she often plowed one of Ralph's three mules from early in the morning to evening, breaking only once to feed herself and the mule. The mule acted as a timepiece, as it would invariably balk and bray at lunchtime.

During the Great Depression, it took a significant amount of sunup-to-sundown manual labor to supply the basic needs of a household. In rural Georgia, kerosene lanterns were the state of the art, and candles were still being made and used. A single farmer could not make all the items needed for a household; thus bartering and trading were commonplace.

During the first few decades of the twentieth century, a cattle farmer would often slaughter a five-hundred-pound calf in the early morning on a late-summer's day. He would lower the calf from the dressing stand onto a buckboard and wrap it in a clean bed sheet. For the remainder of the day, he would make his rounds through the community, trading with other farmers who would select cuts of meat from the carcass. After each cut was removed from the carcass, he would cover it again with the sheet. He, in turn, received farm produce he did not have. To the untrained eye, the products of this delivery system may not have seemed palatable. However, the ready and willing participants in the trade knew supper would be fantastic!

Soft lye soap was made of leftover animal fat—from bacon, salt pork, fatback, and lard—mixed with correct proportions of potash. Outside, a fire was built around a wash pot, using firewood cut and split in the off-season. Special consideration was given to this type of fuel; it needed to be seasoned wood, so it would burn more readily. Fireplaces, wood stoves, and wood cook stoves called for this type of fuel. Even coal was sometimes used. A ridged metal rub board was always a necessary item around the wash pot, where soap and hot water were handy. To have water handy for heating in these larger outside containers it had to drawn from a well or dipped from a spring. Drawing water from the well, or bringing it from the spring in buckets, was another of Ruby Neal's chores.

Chickens were another absolute necessity. Almost everyone had them in their yards. Usually there was a row of hen nests for the layers, nailed to a barn wall. Sometimes a barnyard would have two dozen or more grown chickens scratching the ground for invisible critters for their craws. Fryers were sometimes grown in a waist-high brooder, which was positioned on four legs in the early season, but they were most commonly run down in the yard when dinnertime called for fried chicken. Almost everyone had a favorite brood hen, and so did the rooster. In the late evening, the yard birds would finish filling their craws and could be seen slowly browsing in the same direction. Instinctively, chickens always "come home to roost." When the sun went down, they were supposed to be safe on their roost, but ironically, they were always easier to catch there for sale or trade.

In the latter part of the twentieth century, saturated animal fat began to carry negative connotations for human consumption. Prior to the 1960s, however, fattening animals for slaughter was the farmer's goal. The excessive fat was better for making lard, fatback, candles, sausage, and soap. In fact, a farmer's success at slaughtering time was measured by how many gallons of lard were rendered when the pork cracklings were stewed down in the black wash pot. Likewise, more fat in the milk meant more butter would be churned.

The general rule was to fatten the piglets of early spring to a weight of two hundred pounds or more by winter. During the Great Depression, a very necessary "slop bucket" took the place of today's garbage pail. Recycling may be today's focus, but during the Depression, the slop bucket for the hogs took precedence over the trashcan. On the farm, no labor-intensive food product went to waste. At a minimum, old leftover buttermilk was poured into the five-gallon slop bucket. Red-eye drippings from the skillet, thick gravy, molded biscuits, and any scraps from the breakfast, lunch, and supper tables went into the bucket too. The conveniently packaged world of today did not exist in the year 1930. There was no need for recycling any paper, plastic, or glass containers; neither did such packaging exist for food products. In a trough just over the pigpen fence, horizontal to the ground, lay two boards nailed together in the shape of a *V*, with two short planks across each end. A tin shoot was used to carefully funnel the slop from the bucket into the trough from outside the pen.

Families would kill at least two hogs a year; larger families would slaughter more. During the antebellum years, planters in Greene County conducted hog killings on a grand scale. [101]"The planter had to provide enough meat for his own use and to feed his slaves, so he often killed forty to fifty hogs, and sometimes had two or three

---

[101] T. B. Rice and C. W. Williams, *History of Greene County Georgia*

killings. The first killing was around Thanksgiving, when the first of the cold weather started to settle across the region. A November slaughter was a bit early; a hog's dense hams and shoulders required an extended cold period to rapidly draw out the animal's body heat for preservation purposes. When fall arrived, everyone relished fresh pork. The thick hams and shoulders of the hog were canned or eaten as roasts. Usually, the immediate family and their relatives all worked together to ensure that the first hog was carefully utilized and dispensed.

January was prime weather for killing hogs. When the cold snap came—and it always came—the temperature would barely rise above forty degrees for several consecutive days. Usually, several farmers would meet at a predetermined spot on a creek with plenty of running water. There a wooden scalding box had been built, and the cracks pitched with tar. It would be shielded on the bottom with tin, so the fire beneath would not burn the wooden box. Two chains, which ran parallel to each other across the box, were used to turn the hog in the water. On either side of the scalding box was a platform even with the top of the scalding box. One platform was for receiving, and hog after hog would be dumped into the boiling water as if it were a big bathtub, while someone constantly stoked the fire to keep it scalding hot. At just the right time, the hair would loosen. When it could be snatched from the skin easily, the hog was deemed ready for removal from the scalding box. Then, with the two chains in the hands of strong assistants, the hog was rolled out onto the adjacent platform. Steaming in the cold air, the hog was immediately set upon by numerous hands wielding scraping rocks and razor-sharp knives. As the hog cooled off, buckets filled with the hot water were dashed upon it until all the hair was gone—all of it, from the feet to the ears and around the eyes. No matter what the hog's hair pigment had been, every hog ended up as white and cleanly shaven as if it had been to a barber.

This was something of a turning point in the hog slaughter, from nasty to clean. Fresh buckets of cold creek water would be used to rinse the hog just before it was hoisted and gutted. The necessary downward trend of the hog's body temperature began at this point. Some hogs weighed as much as three hundred pounds, and a hoist was used to draw them up by their hind feet. Everyone who brought a hog also brought as many sharp knives as he or she could gather. A large tub was placed on the ground between the front legs and the hog's jowl. The incision was started at the tail end, as the entrails were rolled into the tub. Nothing was wasted. So much steam was created when the internal heat of the dense hog hit the freezing air that the men could hardly see what they were doing.

Inside the tub were the liver, kidneys, heart, spleen, and chitterlings. These parts of the hog were handed over to the women—and yes, I have seen Mother wash and clean chitterlings, so I know that this was also a part of Ruby Neal's job in the 1930s.

The hog was let down and butterflied open on the back of a wagon. As someone else held the front legs apart, a man with a sharp ax would carefully hack down both sides of the ribcage at the backbone. With each chop the hog would widen a bit more until it lay out flat on its back. By the time every participant's hog was butchered to this point, it was typically late afternoon, and the temperature would have dropped as the sun lowered behind the trees. It was a good stopping point, and everyone went home with his meat in good condition. The wagon with the hog on it would be parked in the coldest spot on the farm for the rest of the night. Often that meant putting it on the roof of an outside building. It would be parked in a place where the rays of the morning sun would not shine upon it. The tenderloin on either side of the backbone was easily removed and made ready for breakfast the next morning.

When morning came, the weather always seemed to be cold and fair. After a fine breakfast of fried tenderloin, hot buttered biscuits, red-eye gravy, scrambled eggs, and coffee, the family was ready to start again on the winter's supply of meat. After the hams and shoulders were removed and taken inside and placed on the dining room table, they were trimmed and shaped for curing—and everyone's hands became numb and cold as ice. The trimmings were cut into chunks of fat and lean and piled into a heap, to be used for sausage. The feet were also sawed off with a handsaw, and the toes were chopped off with an ax. The tips of the toes were thrown away, but the lower eight inches of the pig's feet were pressure-cooked until the meat slipped off the bone.

Old bed sheets with torn toe holes in them were washed thoroughly and saved for this one last purpose. Two sheets torn in half would provide enough wrapping for all four cuts. On each end of the kitchen table, a half sheet was spread and a portion of cure for each cut was mixed. Mama Cleo's recipe contained a half cup of black pepper, a cup of brown sugar, and two cups of salt. Both the skin side and flesh side of the hams were rubbed thoroughly, until the cure disappeared into the ham or shoulder. Then the ham was turned skin-side up and left to drain overnight. The meat was rubbed again in the morning and then wrapped with the half sheet, tied with twine or string, and hung hock-down in the smokehouse. No smoking was necessary for this method, as the pepper in the recipe was not for flavor, but to keep the blowflies away as the spices drew the moisture from the meat. By the end of the cold snap, the meat was nearly ice-cold, through and through. This was a necessary part of the curing process. The meat would cure in four to six weeks.

Obviously, everything that needed to be done to the meat could not be done at one time. Each phase of the work was given its due diligence over a span of several days. Heaping pans of seasoned sausage chunks were set in a cold place to await their turn for the grinder. Mild, medium, and hot sausage recipes were all that was needed. Medium was the hardest to create. When sausage was made hot, the maker never guaranteed *how* hot. But the taste for "medium" varies from person to person. Sage, salt, and red and black pepper were the only seasonings used.

In 1930, a cannery was made available to the public by the county school system in Watkinsville. Farmers could make appointments to have their sausage ground and their meat canned. They returned home with large dishpans full of sausage to be stuffed into long sausage sacks, which were made of old bed sheets and sewn together by a foot-pedal sewing machine.

This time of year was a joyous time of plenty for country people. All the family members and relatives had worked together to have fresh meat for their tables. Now the family's annual harvest was complete, and they could turn their attention toward starting another crop. When the winter weather permitted, more stove wood could be cut to dry. When the planting season arrived, so did a calving dairy cow, a sow with piglets, and baby chicks and clucking hens. The routine repeated itself year after year. During the Great Depression, friends and relatives who lived in town did not eat as well as their rural kin. Visitors from the city could always depend on getting a good meal and hospitality in the country.

Time has a way of devouring farm terminology the same way animals become extinct. Without an effort to record their presence in history, some things become lost forever. Not too far back in human history, animals such as the saber-toothed tiger and the wooly mammoth existed, but now they are extinct, due to either natural or man-induced causes. Within the past century, farming terms such as *hay stocks*, *hands*, and *bundles of fodder mean* have fallen out of use until they mean nothing at all to the twenty-first-century adolescent. To my mother, and to any child of the early twentieth century who lived on a farm, these terms are a reminder of how much hard work had to be done there on a daily basis. Today, the term *horsepower* is used flippantly, without any thought of the origin of its meaning. Before gasoline-powered, mechanized farm machinery became the primary farm implements, horsepower and mules were an absolute necessity. Now the only term salvaged from that era is a number representing how much power is "under the hood."

Another necessary chore my mother performed in the early 1930s was pulling fodder. Efficient farming was a must for survival during the Great Depression. Fresh produce from the garden or field went through its natural process, as it was harvested for food in various stages, depending on whether it was for the table, for trade, or for storage. In mid- to late summer, after the tender corn was boiled on the cob or creamed, the kernels started to harden on the stalk. During the corn's transition into maturity, but before the cornstalk's leaves and shucks became brown, it still contained nutritional value for the mules and horses. With the hardening ear of corn still attached to the stalk, someone would strip the green leaves from the stalk until one hand became full. The last leaf would be wrapped and tucked or wedged between the next available ears of corn. Through another evolution of farm work, four "hands" of fodder would then be gathered together, which would create a bundle. This would be enough for a mule or horse at one feeding.

When mules and horses were worked from sunup to sundown, spare animals would be taken to the fields, along with their food supply. During the plowing or planting season, one mule would consume two bundles of fodder and a few ears of corn, and it would eat chunks of salt like candy on a daily basis.

After the modern transition to the tractor, the farmer only needed to take his lunch and a can of gasoline with him.

While fodder was required for the plowing stock, cows preferred hay for roughage. Good hay is derived from various species of plant life and grasses, but the gathering process for fodder and hay was different during the Great Depression. When the weather was fair and hot, hay would be cut using a sickle and left lying in the field to dry and cure, trapping the green nutrients inside its stems and leaves. When the barn loft was full of hay and fodder, hay stocks were used to preserve it for early use before winter. During the Great Depression, when hay was cut and before the next rain could come, the farmer would hitch up a mule and wagon, and with his pitchfork, he would pile as much loose hay onto the wagon as would stay there on its trip to the barnyard. Once at the barnyard, he would offload the wagon with his fork, piling the hay up and against a tall pole or "stock" that he had set into the ground. He would pile up the hay until the pole disappeared into the mound and then he would cover the mound with a canvas. Early in the twentieth century, stocks of hay were as common in the barnyard as rolls of hay are today.

A "fresh cow" was a farmer's dairy cow—usually a small brown Jersey—that had recently calved. This event created a higher volume of milk, sometimes gallons per day. This increased lactation would dwindle during gestation. The cow would be allowed to dry up about three months before calving again. The next cow up would then be milked the same way until the previous one calved again.

The colostrum required for baby calves was not palatable; it was left for the calf for several days before regular milking began. At the beginning of the milking period, there would be more milk, but it was thinner, with less butterfat; soon, however, rich yellow milk would come from the Jersey cow. This meant that cream, butter, buttermilk, and sweet milk would be plenteous for the family. From my own experience milking five such cows by hand on a daily basis, I can report that the rich yellow butterfat comes at the end of the cow's milking. Thus, it is important to completely strip the yellow butterfat from the cow's udder.

When the daily chores directed toward food essentials were finished, attention could be focused on other necessities, such as clothing. Mama Cleo was handy with a needle and thread and the sewing machine. What new dresses there were came from bought material that was stitched together according to patterns made from newspapers. Mother would stand as still as she could, and Mama Cleo would cut the paper, which had been pinned together around her body's outline. Then, using the paper pattern, Mama Cleo would cut the new material to Mother's approximate dimensions.

Mother's School Picture

Same Building Today

The Merging of Two Families

I n the course of events from about 1930 to 1932, two houses next to each other on Elder Mill Road became vacant. The house nearer the covered bridge sat upon a 180-acre farm, which Ralph Hardigree purchased. Next door, Nando Miller lived in a farmhouse on land belonging to John Clovis Saxon. The house came up for rent when Nando Miller moved out, conveniently providing a residence for the Robert Lavender family. This move would place the family in close proximity to the land that Papa would be sharecropping. Initially, this rural setting, on a dirt road in southern Oconee County, would be the first of several home sites for Clifford and Ruby Neal, all of them within a three-mile radius. Times were hard, but the Lavenders and the Hardigees became close friends and neighbors.

Electricity had not yet come to rural areas like this one; that luxury was still limited to town dwellers. However, things changed around 1935, when Franklin D. Roosevelt was shocked by the disparity between the electric bills for his Warm Springs, Georgia, cottage and his New York home. As a result, his administration developed the Rural Electric Administration. If the large utilities were unable to provide electricity to all Americans, the government would now take an active role to see that everyone could have it. When the REA first provided this invisible source of power, it was provided through distribution lines along the main roadways.

At that time Dad was twenty-three, Uncle Carl twenty, Uncle Clarence sixteen, and Aunt Hazel fourteen, the same age as Ruby Neal. After a couple of farming seasons, Carl married Lizzie Ruth Fambrough, but he continued farming with Dad and Papa for several years, as they helped each other make it through the hard times.

From this setting came two statements about my father that our immediate family has heard time and again: "Clifford robbed the cradle!" Mother always told us four brothers over and over, "Cliff had to wait for me to grow up." Between the two statements, readers can draw their own conclusions about the ebb and flow of country living between these two neighboring families. A very special relationship developed between a twenty-three-year-old man and the fourteen-year-old girl he saw on a daily basis, a girl already doing a man's work.

The families shared farm implements, mules, and even labor when Mama Cleo or Ralph was sick. That's what neighbors did in those days. Mother earned the respect of the Lavender family when they saw her plowing fields, milking the cows, and slopping the hogs. With three scrapping boys, Mama Lavender felt sorry for Ruby Neal, but in a very respectful way. Ruby was doing what was expected of her in the Ralph Hardigree family. Dad, of course, had a special respect for and interest in the young girl who had become his baby sister's friend. I saw forty-eight years of their chiding, kidding, and laughing with one another, so I can well imagine what went on in their lives between 1932 and 1935. With Dad and her in the barn alone, he might have said, "Here! Let me do that!" as she unharnessed the mules. "You feed the cow." Mother has said that during those years she looked up to Clifford and Carl as the big brothers she never had. Aunt Ebbie, Ralph's baby sister, once said to Mother, "You be good to that Cliff. He has always put you first in everything."

Two miles away, Antioch Christian Church had been the hub of religious, social, and community activity in that region of Georgia for the past century. Founded in 1822, it already held the distinction of being the oldest Christian denomination church in the state.

For the sake of clarity I must inject here that Lutheran, Methodist, Presbyterian, Baptist, etc. are all Christian denominations. In 1793 James O'Kelly started the American Reformation movement when he and approximately a third of the annual Methodist Convention split from the Methodist denomination. Next came the Cane Ridge Revivals in Kentucky in 1801. As new churches were planted they inevitably had an issue with what the distinction in their name might be. In this area of Georgia during early colonization, the exact spot where Antioch Christian Church now stands, they named the log meetinghouse Old Republican. The parishioners were first called O'Kellites and Bible Totin' Christians. Later, after the influence of Campbell and Stone was injected to the movement, the members were called Campbellites and Stoneites in a derisive manner.

In 1822 Old Republican was outgrown, and a new structure was built beside it. The name issue came up again. Nathan Smith, a well-known and effective missionary from the membership, tried to help settle the issue when he suggested that they be called Christians. It was accepted and the new structure was called the Christian Church at Old Republican. Afterwards, many other sister churches sprung up throughout the region, such as Watkinsville Christian Church, Union Christian Church, and others.

Every denomination carries an implication within its name. Our founders simply chose the Christian implication.

During the first few days of recruit training for the navy, we lined up to receive our dog tags. These small aluminum plates were stamped with the serviceman's name, service number, and religion. The sailor taking down the information asked my denomination. I replied, "Christian." He barked back, "Ahh hell, man! We all are Christian." He was seeking Protestant, Catholic, etc. to select the proper clergyman should I ever require last rights.

In 1926, the *Christian Endeavor Guide* was published, becoming a moral and spiritual guideline for youth in the church. The program was a great success within the denomination and provided a purpose for the meetings of its young people. Before electricity became available, a single chandelier was used to light the early-evening programs, and the walls of the sanctuary were lined with kerosene lanterns.

The first members of the Robert Lavender family to transfer from the Methodist denomination to the Christian denomination were all his children in August 1933, three years before Mother and Dad married in August1936. Papa and Mama joined in 1941.

On the Fourth of July, 1934, Mama Cleo was put in traction for eight weeks as a result of back problems. This created a need for Ruby Neal to step up and fill the gap in the chores. The Lavender family was particularly concerned for Ruby Neal as they witnessed the extreme conditions placed upon her. Sara Webb Hardigree was having a birthday picnic at Reginald Hardigree's pond, so Aunt Hazel extended the invitation to Ruby Neal. Mother was so overwhelmed with her family's laundry that she declined the invitation at first. But Aunt Hazel insisted, telling her that Mama Lavender had prepared enough food for all of them.

At the party, sheets were spread on the ground and the food arranged on them. Some people swam, but others, like Mother, didn't. Helen, Aunt Hazel's soon-to-be sister-in-law, hosted the picnic. Later in the afternoon, Helen said, "Come on up the hill, and I'll put some records on the Victrola!" The young people danced and danced all evening. Later on, the dance party turned into a prom party, and at the age of sweet sixteen, Ruby Neal was asked by my dad to go to prom with him. "That's how we got started going together," Mother told us later. That evening Dad also asked her if she would go to Christian Endeavor with him. Mother agreed that she would when she could. For fifteen months they courted in this manner, country-style.

By 1930, the automobile was becoming a necessity for almost everyone. Second-hand vehicles of the 1920s, the kind with side curtains, were becoming accessible to rural folks who couldn't afford to purchase a new car. Uncle Carl bought his first used car about 1932, after his marriage to Lizzie Ruth Fambrough. About a year later, Uncle Jerry Hardigree became a Ford man and started his professional mechanical career by stripping down an early-model Ford. (This transformation made it an early hot rod.) A used Buick became Papa Lavender's first family car. Mother recalls that all three were early models with side curtains.

After the prom party, Dad broke up with an older woman named Lita Turner and put his total focus on the girl next door. He was twenty-five. Throughout that summer and the next year, they walked and talked on the roads near home. They often met at the end of the day, when they both were tired and dirty from working in the fields, but they were satisfied just to sit together in the front porch swing at sunset.

In the summer of 1935, Ralph purchased Mother's books for her final year of school, the eleventh grade, as school would start back in September. But on October 6, after Christian Endeavor, Dad asked Mother to ride down to the river to see the construction of the new bridge that crossed over the Oconee River into Greene County. There he proposed to her. She did not answer him right away, and this concerned him.

A week later, Dad came in from the fields, tired and dirty and somewhat blue, and sat in the swing with Mom. "Well," he asked, "have you made up your mind?"

Mother smiled at him and said, "I reckon I will."

That gave Dad a real shot of adrenaline. As Mother told me later, "He was a happy man."

Dad and Mother made their plans in privacy, setting a date that was contingent upon the crops and their "lay-by times." They selected August 3, during the Antioch Revival of the next year.

To say the least, Papa Ralph's personality was a bit high-strung and his mental health beginning to deteriorate. Mother and Dad decided that their engagement would be a bit too much for him. Though Clifford was considered all right for a friend and neighbor, Ralph and Cleo thought he was too old for Ruby Neal. Dad and Mother already knew what Ralph's response to their engagement would be. So, inconspicuously, instead of an engagement ring, Dad bought Mother an Elgin wristwatch, which she wore for many years. During their ten-month engagement, when Mother was sick or under the weather or simply inaccessible, Dad would drop a love letter in the mailbox as he passed by on his way to the fields. Thus, all their plans were made in privacy during the normal routine of country living as next-door neighbors.

The week of July 31, 1936, court was being held for the trial of a chicken thief against whom Ralph had pressed charges. That timing created a serious problem, as it conflicted with Clifford and Ruby Neal's application for a marriage license. Coincidentally, the same justice who had married Cleo and Ralph nineteen years earlier was handling the younger couple's marriage application. When the justice, Mr. Fullilove, looked at the application, he grew concerned. "Clifford," he asked, "is she of age?"

Sheepishly, Dad replied, "Uh, I think so."

The justice said, "Let me see," and he counted on his fingers. "I married Ralph and Cleo in 1917, and I don't think she is of age. We'll have to post this license."

The couple's hearts sank as the justice made his way toward the bulletin board. Afraid that Ralph would see their license while attending court over the chicken theft, Dad asked the justice to put it behind some of the other postings, in a place where it could not be seen.

For the next three days when Ralph would go to court, Mother and Dad held their breath, dreading the worst.

Finally August 3 arrived, and final preparations for their elopement began. Dad had asked Mama Lavender if he and Ruby Neal could stay with her and Papa until the crop was harvested sometime in November. Mama Lavender was very pleased with the arrangements and agreed that Mom and Dad could stay in a vacant room across the hall from Mama and Papa Lavender.

The plan on August 3, 1936, was for Aunt Hazel, Uncle Jerry, Uncle Carl, Aunt Lizzie Ruth, and Dad to come by Ralph and Cleo's house and invite Ruby Neal to ride to the American Legion pool in Athens. Their excuse for going was to watch the students swim, which they did—but only after Ruby's six soon-to-be in-laws went on a shopping spree for the wedding party. Mother had transformed her pocketbook into a miniature suitcase, as it was packed with her gown and underwear and anything else she thought she might need for the evening. Mother still chuckles, "I was so afraid Mama was going to notice my bulging purse as I was leaving."

After the party left Ralph's house and the dust had settled on Elder Mill Road, Dad borrowed ten dollars from Uncle Carl to purchase Mother's orange blossom wedding band from Fricketts Department Store on Clayton Street in Athens. With the five dollars Aunt Lizzie Ruth had given her for a wedding present, Mother bought a blue crepe dress to go with her white sandals. When Mother told the story later, she would be sure to add, "If you marry in blue, you will always be true." Dad wore his white buckskin shoes that he had cleaned before the ceremony, which was scheduled for six o'clock that evening.

They finished their shopping two hours early, so in keeping with their word, the wedding party sat in the shade on the bleachers by the legion pool. As they watched the college students swim, the wedding party shared a half-gallon of ice cream using flat wooden spoons. "I still have those spoons," Mother says.

After the ceremony, the new in-laws headed back to south Oconee County and the Antioch Revival. As they drove by Ralph and Cleo's, Uncle Carl deliberately stayed down on the main road, slowing to a stop and blowing his horn to get the attention of Aunt Agnes. Making sure that Aunt Agnes saw him, Dad placed a letter into Ralph's mailbox telling Papa Ralph and Mama Cleo how much he loved my mother and that he would always take good care of her. Aunt Agnes, who knew something was up, ran to the mailbox and quickly delivered the letter to Mama Cleo. Papa Ralph was on the back porch, shaving in preparation for the revival, when the news broke inside and mayhem ensued. When Papa Ralph asked what all the fuss was about, Aunt Agnes, nearly overwhelmed by excitement, repeated over and over, "Sister and Clifford got married!"

In utter dejection, Papa Ralph threw his straight razor into the shaving water and said, "We just won't go to church!"

The younger siblings, now adamant about going to the revival, began begging, "We want to see them!"—"As if we had changed," Mother later said, laughing.

In those days, the front two corners of the sanctuary were filled with short pews set adjacent to each other. As a result of their positioning, the choir on one side and the patrons on the other side faced one another. The wedding party took their seats with the choir, and Uncle Thomas, Uncle Gene, and Aunt Agnes—all under the age of fourteen—sat across from the wedding party, snickering and grinning like the cat that had swallowed the canary.

After church, the wedding party dispersed and Mom and Dad spent their honeymoon night in the room across the hall from Mama and Papa Lavender. Late into the next morning of August 4, 1936, loud squawking awakened Mother and Dad. Aunt Hazel and Uncle Jerry had arrived in time to run down a yard bird, and a fine brunch of southern fried chicken was lovingly prepared for the newlyweds' first meal.

Mama and Papa invited Mother and Dad to stay on a while longer than they had originally planned, until after the first hog killing after Thanksgiving. Preparations were also being made for them to move into the old sharecropper's house that sat off the road on Ralph's farm. The most pressing chore was the joint effort of processing the first fresh meat of the season. Papa and Mama Lavender gave the newlyweds their first hog after Thanksgiving, and by November 30, the family had all their sausage stuffed in sacks and hung in the smokehouse. Plenteous cans of cracklings and lard, salted meat, and cured hams and shoulders were finished and in the smokehouse only yards away from the bedroom where Clifford and Ruby Neal slept.

The old-timers knew they could always depend on the necessary cold snap just after Thanksgiving of each year for the first hog killing, and they were not disappointed in 1936. A terrible ice storm blew in as the Lavender family finished processing the first hog of the year. Uncle Clarence was concerned about a molted hen that had lost all her feathers just before the ice storm began. Realizing that the hen would freeze to death before morning, he warmed a rock in the fireplace, wrapped the hen and the rock together in a towel, and put the bundled bird in the smokehouse for the night.

Later Mother noticed light through their bedroom window, and she peered out to see who was arriving, but the light was not from automobile headlights. To her terror and dismay, she realized that the smokehouse was fully engulfed in flames. The alarm went out over a hand-cranked wall phone, and immediately the neighbors began to arrive and assist in putting out the fire, forming a bucket brigade to keep the nearest side of the Lavender house from also igniting. The neighbors said if it had not been for the ice that was frozen to that side of the house, the house would have caught on fire before they arrived.

Needless to say, both sides of the family were devastated over the loss. They quickly joined together to plan an alternate strategy to provide the necessities for the newlyweds.

Papa Ralph gave Mother and Dad a fresh milk cow, with a small Jersey bull calf named Bimbo beside her, since their main meat supply had gone up in flames. Bimbo would be butchered a few months later. Everyone pitched in to make sure there was enough for the newlyweds to eat. Dad would pick gallons of dewberries and blackberries in late spring for jam and cobblers. There was plenty of wheat and corn left from the previous year, and a mill nearby. Mother always chuckles when she tells the story, and each time she declares, "Those were some good ol' times. I believe we were happier then than folks are now. Folks now have so much they don't seem to be happy with anything."

By then Mother was already pregnant with my eldest brother, Roger. Just below the two main houses, but farther back off the road on the Hardigree farm, was a frame sharecropper's house. It still had some redeemable qualities but was rapidly falling into disrepair. This was Ruby Neal and Clifford's first home together. Electricity had not yet come to the area when they moved into the house late in 1936. It is hard to imagine the condition of this old house, considering that they thought they had moved up in the world when their next move was into the Allis Elder house. The walls of that house were not insulated, and chickens could be seen through the floor. Roger was the first of Mother and Dad's four boys, and unlike Bobby and me, Roger and Jimmie each had his own distinctive birthplace in a sharecropper's house. The last of us brothers, Bobby and I, shared the same address at the Big Springs place, though we were the first of the four boys to be born at Saint Mary's Hospital on Milledge Avenue in Athens. In 1951, before I was old enough to remember, we moved into the Hardigree-Holbrook house. The family would forever call it home, as it became our primary destination after all the brothers had traveled the world over.

In 1938, a year or so before Granny died, the golden age of radio was at its pinnacle. It was about 8:30 on a Sunday evening, October 30, when *The War of the Worlds* was broadcast nationwide without interruption. Orson Welles had no way of knowing the panic that would ensue among millions of Americans throughout the country.

The listening public still had not learned to distinguish fact from fiction, as it was argued in the 1940 book about the case, *The Invasion from Mars: A Study in the Psychology of Panic.* The radio story was given play-by-play narration without interruption. Uncle Clarence was sent up the hill to notify Mother and Dad, who were next door at Ralph Hardigree's house. Clarence shouted, "The most awful thing imaginable has happened! The radio is broadcasting the end of the world!" Mother and Dad snatched up Roger, only six months old at the time, and down the hill the family ran. The Lavender and Hardigree families met at the Lavender household, where they listened to the radio and awaited their doom. Mother has often said that she did not care about herself but felt very sorry for her infant son. She said she expected a ball of fire to crash through the house at any moment.

There were descriptions of slimy monsters with black eyes and tentacles exiting their crafts with pulsating ray guns, and thousands of people in Chicago and St. Louis running for their lives. (That part was actually true.) Granny was eighty-eight years old, so this news was kept from her. Grandma Bessie was the excitable sort, and because of her rapid pulse, she was given special attention. Not until the broadcast broke for station identification did the alarmed family—and the American public—know it was fiction.

At times, Ralph's heart would soften toward Dad, and he would lend the newlyweds his mules to raise two crops while they resided in the sharecropper's house on his farm. But in 1939, Mother and Dad decided to cut ties with Ralph and move into the Allis Elder house, which sat directly on the land that Dad would be farming. By this time they had their own hog, a milk cow, and chickens, with a garden nearby.

Between the years 1933 and 1938, Allis-Chalmers tractors were becoming popular among the small farmers who were still using mules. The WC model had been on the market for several years and had caught the eye of Papa Lavender. Between him and his two eldest sons, he thought, an investment in one of those modern marvels would cut their field labor in half. By 1938, instead of taking mules, fodder, a wagon, a plow, and their farmers' lunch to the field, they had to take only their lunch and a can of gasoline. Ground preparation was now so easy for them that farmers from miles around would come to see Uncle Carl and Dad plow around the clock in back-to-back shifts, as one brother would rest on the ground while the other brother plowed into the night. The small mule farmers in the community also hired the brothers for this type of ground preparation.

About this same time, an opportunity came along for Uncle Carl and Dad to work as carpenters. Bill Mathis owned a substantial construction company and needed to build one hundred houses in Macon, Georgia. The men agreed on an arrangement that balanced their farming obligations with their construction jobs. Dad and Carl left for Macon in Carl's car. The pay was good, but they only got to come home on the weekends in the off-season.

It was very depressing for the two sad pairs when the brothers left for Macon early each Monday morning. The men asked the foreman if each of them could build a temporary shanty on the vacant land between construction sites, as some of the other workers were doing. Then their wives could travel with them back and forth from Watkinsville to Macon and be with their husbands. Their request was approved. Using scrap lumber not needed on the construction site, they built their shanties on the vacant lots. During the years 1939–41, they lived alternately between Oconee County, where they farmed with Papa Lavender, and the Macon construction site.

It was during this time in Macon that Roger, age three, wandered off with the "dog man," who was also the plumber for the construction project. The man roamed the construction sites and gave suckers to the children as a pack of dogs followed him. Roger had always loved dogs, and before Mother knew it, he was gone. She was hysterical, as any new mother would be. She searched the area over until she finally found him and "gave him a good spanking," as she later said. She put him in his crib, where he sobbed and cried himself to sleep—but, she said, "He never wandered off again."

In May 1940, Phillip Hardigree had business in Florida, and the Hardigree-Holbrook house was left vacant for a short period of time. Aunt Trudie and Uncle Henry Barnett were its last occupants, and because of an insurance clause, the house needed to be occupied. Aunt Trudie asked Mother and Dad if they would housesit for a few days until Phillip returned from Florida.

They agreed and moved a few basic housekeeping necessities from the Allis Elder house, using a custom-made platform Dad had built for the back of the tractor. This platform provided the first motorized transportation for Clifford and Ruby Neal. Riding the platform was easier than harnessing the mules. They were making a slow transition from mules and wagons to the mechanized luxury of gasoline-powered transportation. There were only a couple of miles between where the Allis Elder house was located and the Hardigree-Holbrook house on Greensboro Road.

It was May 2, 1940, and Mother and Dad had just made the temporary move into the Hardigree-Holbrook house, when what the old-timers called "blackberry winter" occurred. There were three chimneys and five fireplaces in the big house; those five fireplaces warmed five rooms. Since it was the middle of spring, Mother and Dad had no way of knowing that Phillip's second wife, Edna, had already stuffed each of the chimneys with sacks of wheat straw. This was done in an attempt to keep the droppings of chimney swifts from making a mess on the clean, whitewashed brick hearths.

During my parents' cold tractor ride from the Allis Elder house a mile away, the bottom dropped out of the thermometer. Evening was approaching, and they shuffled into the cold house with Roger, who was wrapped in a blanket. The first order of business was to start a fire. The obvious then happened: the house filled with smoke, and great balls of fire fell onto the hearth and rolled out into the room as the soot caught on fire. As they worked to put out the fire from the wheat straw, Uncle Carl drove up with the bad news that Granny had died. Of course, that changed the evening's plans. As tough as it was, Dad, Mother, and Roger left with Uncle Carl to find the nearest telephone in Watkinsville, so they could notify other family members. Then they made the trip to Crawford, Georgia, to tell Granny's brother, Uncle Jim Roe.

During their short stay in the big house, Dad used the tractor and platform to carry slop for the hogs, and anything else that needed transporting between the two residences. After some insistence from Aunt Trudie, Phillip later paid Mother a meager $100 for their trouble.

Dad, Mother, Uncle Carl, Aunt Lizzie Ruth, and Roger were in Macon on December 7, 1941, when the news broke about Pearl Harbor. The men in the family worked for several more months until the draft was in full swing and every able-bodied man was put into a classification that would most benefit the requirements of the nation. Dad and Uncle Carl's classification was IIC, which was "registrant deferred in support of agriculture." Farm units were also required for this classification, so Mama Lavender told her young men to come home and get their units together. Besides, Mother was pregnant with Jimmie.

Dad salvaged the lumber from their shanties and remodeled their bedroom at the Allis Elder place, making an airtight bedroom and nursery in preparation for Jimmie's arrival.

On April 15, 1943, Dad had planned to plow the bottoms on Ralph's farm, but the night before there had been a bitter freeze. Papa Lavender came over and offered to plow the bottom land, saying that Dad should stay close to home since Mother's time was so near.

Dad and Mother had eight rows of potatoes that had already put out leaves. Papa told Dad to cut off the potato tops and cover them with soil so they could recover from the freeze. Dad was doing just what his father had suggested when Mother got the bellyache, and he left to get Dr. Kenimar in Bishop, Georgia.

The next year there came an opportunity to move into a better sharecropper's house on the main road. These old homes on the main road were the first homes in the area to be supplied with electricity; wires were run through the attics to provide a single droplight and socket for each room. These light sockets initially held light bulbs. Later, the light bulbs were replaced with screw-in receptacles with a plug-in on each side and the light bulb connection on the bottom. This arrangement provided electricity not only for light, but also for the first appliances, such as electric irons, mixers, fans, and toasters. Later these old houses were rewired to better safety standards. Newly built homes were wired with built-in receptacles.

The farm where their house stood became known as "the Jake Norton place," named for the man who bought it after Mother and Dad had occupied the house for just one growing season. They liked the Norton house and farm, but now they had to move down Greensboro Road about three miles, to the vacant Big Springs place that sat right off the road. It too was wired for lights.

So once again Mother and Dad moved, for the fourth time in eight years, seeking out better living conditions for their family.

The First and Last Washwoman

C ast iron wash pots, tubs, and washboards were still commonly used by families making the transition from manual labor to a more electrically mechanized way of washing clothes. In 1944, Mother and Dad were already using a seven-gallon wash pot, but they purchased a twenty-gallon pot from Mrs. Mae Anderson, my wife's grandmother, in Watkinsville. Mother has given us both the pots as heirlooms, and Cheryl has said jokingly that the only reason she married me was to get back the wash pot. We are especially attached to the twenty-gallon pot and use it primarily to cook large quantities of hash and stews, which take on a distinctive, wood-smoked flavor. The twenty-gallon wash pot would become the center of a tragic accident at the Big Springs place.

Fortunately for Mother, Dad, and the family, they found the Big Springs place on the main road available for rent in 1944. By the spring of 1945, Mother was six months pregnant with Bobby. Ever so gradually, Mother and Dad were seeking out a better financial life for their growing family. Dad still borrowed Papa Lavender's car for doctor's visits and necessary errands; it would be five more years before the family could afford a pickup truck.

Papa Ralph's mental health continued to deteriorate to the point that his visits to the doctors in Milledgeville could not sustain him for any length of time, so his hospital stay became permanent. Mama Cleo moved to Watkinsville, living with Uncle Thomas until the 1950s, when Dad and some others built a small, two-bedroom house on Uncle Thomas's property. Mother and Dad were given the cows from Papa Ralph's farm, and Dad began to sell "B-grade" milk.

A-grade vs. B-grade milk had to do with the bacteria count, implying that the A-grade milk had less bacteria in it. The way the milk was collected from the farm had a great deal to do with this classification. Hand milked, strained, and put in a five-gallon can was the method that classified B-grade milk. Mother often rode with the milkman, Mr. Thornton, as a means of transportation into town to see the doctor or for other necessary appointments. Their income from milk sales helped to pay the light bill.

Dad obviously could not plant in the winter and fall, so during the periods he did not have to tend to a crop or its preparation there was a break. During this break from the fields, Dad had piled a large supply of firewood near the kitchen and washing area of the Big Springs house. Now Roger was in school and it was time for planting, and Dad needed gasoline for the tractor. He could only run that errand after he provided a ride for the young black woman who was to help mother do the wash. After returning with the washwoman, Dad picked up two-year-old Jimmie, who had been sitting on the tractor tire near the wash pot, and the two of them went for gasoline in Papa's car.

Mother was inside hanging curtains on this bright and sunny spring day. The washwoman was outside, attempting to start a fire around the black wash pot so she could boil the dirty clothes in lye-soapy water. Within minutes after Dad left with Jimmie, Mother heard a loud explosion and went to the door, only to see the washwoman engulfed in flames. The woman ran toward the house as the flames leaped above her head; consequently she breathed in the flames and collapsed on the porch at the door. Mother used water to put out the fire and butter to help with the burns, but it was immediately obvious that the burns were much more serious than anything a home remedy could treat. The washwoman struggled with her last words, saying, "Go tell my people."

Black Wash Pot

Six months pregnant with Bobby, Mother ran to the main road to flag down anyone who might be coming along. In those days, from the top of the hill of the Big Springs place, Mother could see in both directions for up to a mile. As Dad and Jimmie returned from their errand, Dad saw Mother at a distance and knew something was wrong.

Dad went to Mother's side as she broke down, explaining what had happened. "I went down the old road and told Uncle John," she said. "Uncle John had to go to Watkinsville to Spec Downs at the fork to send for emergency help."

Dad took Mother to the house and parked in the front yard so she would not be traumatized any further. The old-timers later said they were glad that Mother did not lose the pregnancy and that Bobby was not "marked" in any way.

Mother was then taken away from the fray and put to bed as the emergency personnel, such as they were, took the washwoman to Saint Mary's Hospital on Milledge Avenue in Athens—the same hospital where Bobby and I would later be born. But on this tragic day, at about one o'clock in the afternoon of the year 1944, with the world at war, the family's first and the last washwoman passed away.

It became painfully apparent to my dad at this juncture that Mother needed a modern appliance that could help lessen the burden of her chores. A Maytag washer with an attached ringer was chosen. Before I was a twinkle in Dad's eye, he purchased the Maytag washer for my mother, and it served the family for many years. Though the water still had to be hauled in, the electric washer reduced the amount of her physical labor.

I remember being a small boy at the Hardigree-Holbrook house and seeing the four-legged Maytag washer and ringer sitting on the back porch, near the place where we took our baths in a tin tub. If anyone drove into the yard while we were bathing, we would streak naked through the house. This would leave a trail of wet footprints that led to a shivering and soaked child waiting for a towel.

At the Big Springs place, life for Mom and Dad consisted of farming and housework until three in the afternoon. Roger and

Jimmie were bused to and from school. Dad took a part-time job at Dairy Pak, working the evening shift; he would catch a ride into town with their next-door neighbor, Robert Elder. But the relatively mundane lifestyle Mother and Dad had experienced during the first fifteen years of their marriage was about to change.

A House Becomes a Home

❦ ——— ❧

B y 1950, our family at the Big Springs place had grown from four to six. Mother's grandparents' house, the Hardigree-Holbrook house, belonged to Phillip and his wife Lula, their only child. Subsequently, when Lula died, Phillip held only a child's interest in the farm, and his children held the controlling interest. In 1951, after Phillip's family had left the nest, the house became vacant and Phillip decided to rent it out. But Aunt Trudy confronted her father, saying that if anyone was given an opportunity to live in the house, it should be his granddaughter, Ruby Neal, and Clifford, with their four small children. One day, after some deliberation, and while Dad was still working at Dairy Pak, Phillip paid a visit to Mother at the Big Springs place.

Hesitantly he said, "Hmm, hmm, if you and Clifford want to work the Holbrook farm on halves with me, I'll come down with my truck tomorrow and help you move."

There was no way to notify Dad of the good news, so Mother immediately began packing for the next day's move. So in 1951, the Hardigree-Holbrook house became a home for our family. For ten years, Dad sharecropped with Phillip and paid rent, which left very little from the annual farm income. If there was any livestock production over that from a single milk cow, a hog, and a few chickens, Phillip expected to receive half.

After living in five different sharecropper's houses, Mother and Daddy finally were able to rent the large, five-bedroom house Phillip had built for Lula in 1908. Fortunately for me, it became the only home I ever knew as a child. We children dared not destroy the countless hundreds of cancelled checks—ranging from a few dollars to several thousand dollars—that we found in the numerous satchels and suitcases in a back bedroom. As a small boy in 1960, before Phillip passed away, I would sit among the suitcases and rummage through the cancelled checks. I marveled in awe at my great-grandfather's vast wealth.

With the extra forty-one acres Dad had to farm, he finally bought a new 1950 Chevrolet pickup truck. He then went into full-time row cropping. But on the horizon was the necessary trend of the two-income household. From 1951 to 1956, the family of six lived, loved, and worked, keeping the forty-one-acre Holbrook house and farm in the family.

From the time Roger was old enough to drive the pickup and help Dad in the fields, Mother and Dad gave him permission to take all the boys to the movies in Athens on the weekends. During the planting season, Dad would keep the older brothers out of school a few days so he could get the crop planted. Each one of us brothers grew into more responsible chores every year. Ultimately, that meant that after milking the cows, slopping the hogs, and churning the butter, we would head to the fields with Dad. In preparation for this trip to the field, we would load the half-ton pickup with a ton of fertilizer in hundred-pound bags. We would offload it one bag at a time into two five-gallon buckets. Dad would estimate the length of the rows he was planting and then position the pickup loaded with fertilizer at the halfway mark. He would chuckle at his young sons as they strained to lift the fifty-pound buckets over their heads and into the cultivator hopper. When things were going smoothly in the fields and the equipment was working correctly, Dad would roll a cigarette from his Prince Albert tobacco can. With the cigarette in the corner of a grin as broad as Texas, he would shout above the tractor engine, "Pour it in, boys, I ain't got time to stop!" All four boys went through the same apprenticeship as we grew into and out of the row-cropping cultivation process.

In the early 1950s at the Holbrook farm, our family observed many of the old-time farming methods. Because of Dad's agreement with Phillip, little improvement to the house and outbuildings was risked. Dad was not financially able to make improvements at that time. However, if Dad had made improvements to the property that he was only renting, Phillip might not have renewed the agreement between them and sought better terms with another sharecropper at our family's expense.

The numerous dilapidated outbuildings were prime habitats for nesting hens. When I was five or six years of age, searching for the birds became one of my favorite pastimes with Mother. I would tug on her apron and beg, "Come on, Muh, let's go find a hen nest."

Among the outbuildings was the family privy, which was visible to anyone driving along the highway. Thus it was very obvious that the Hardigee-Holbrook house was not plumbed for running water, as it had no modern bathroom. All the brothers were embarrassed about our privy status, since we had to ride the school bus every day. In 1960 most of the children on the bus had a bathroom in their homes. We constantly pressed our parents for a bathroom, but until 1965 we were confined to bathing in tin tubs and, when nature called, dashing through the snow.

The hand-dug well was immediately down the back steps and a few yards to the right. The well box was four feet high, with double-hinged flapping covers. It was rigged with a pulley and chain to draw a two-gallon bucket of water from about forty feet down. With Phillip's permission, and about the time I became tall enough and strong enough to draw water, Dad installed an electric water pump. Soon afterward he bought a water heater and plumbed the back porch with two faucets. One was for cold water and one was for hot, so we could fill the Maytag washer on the back porch. Later came the kitchen sink.

1957 was a good year for our family there on the Holbrook farm. Dad was literally in his prime when it came to farming, at times making more than a bale of cotton to the acre. Also in 1957, just after I started school, Snow White Laundry at Five Points in Athens hired

Mother. She worked there faithfully for fifteen years, contributing greatly to the financial well-being of our family. Because of her we could afford so many things we'd never had before. School supplies, clothes, furniture, and supplies the farm could not produce were just a few things she provided, making it easier for us. This was also the year the family bought its very first automobile—and a fine car it was. It was a 1957 green-and-white Ford Fairlane with gold trim, fender skirts, and whitewall tires. Roger used it a few times for dating, but Jimmie and Bobby utilized it best. (Soon after Roger graduated from high school, he enlisted in the navy.) Mother mostly drove it to and from work in Athens. She and Dad could now take the first of what would be many trips to Daytona Beach, Florida, leaving us boys to take care of the farm.

The headwaters of Wildcat Creek start on the Holbrooks' original forty-one acres, where my brother Jimmie's Little Creek Farm is today. The high banks of the spring were formed from drainage off Mrs. Sara M. Downs's acreage. These high banks became a substantial source of the white mud the family used to whitewash the hearths of the five fireplaces in the big house. The chore of collecting the mud in the whitewash bucket and whitewashing the hearths became my responsibility.

My personal memories of Phillip Hardigree are like fleeting vapors; he was simply the old man who lived next door and drove a red Dodge pickup. My most poignant memory of him involves a cold Saturday morning in 1958. From less than a quarter mile away, walking south on Greensboro Highway, came Phillip Hardigree—a bent, gray man in a gray overcoat with a walking cane. He was halfway between his house, at the corner of Astondale Road, and our home before we recognized him. I heard Dad tell Mom, "He's come to collect the rent."

I had just finished taking out the ashes, whitewashing the kitchen hearth, and stoking the fire when my parents invited him in to sit by the fireplace. He sat down in a straight chair, huddled up close to the fire with his feet on the rapidly drying hearth, and held out his hands to warm them. Before too much was said, he let go of a long stream of tobacco juice that half missed the fire as it streamed across my freshly whitewashed hearth. It is not an endearing memory of my great-grandfather, but it is poignant.

My three brothers and I were constantly into some kind of playful mischief. During the short periods of time when we weren't working, we might find ourselves shooting flip staffs, made from a branch where the limbs forked. We would cut thin strips of rubber off an old, cast-aside tire inner tube and firmly secure two of the ends on each of the forked limbs. On the two other ends of rubber strips we secured the leather tongue from an old shoe. All we needed then was just the right-sized pebble or rock to use as a projectile. At times we found ourselves firing away at one another or getting into a walnut war. Generally this meant the three younger brothers would gang up on Roger. Being the smallest and the baby of the family, I did not pose a threat and was not a target in these skirmishes.

Roger was in the first class that graduated from the new Oconee High School. For his graduation present, Mother bought him—as she later would buy for all of us—a nice wristwatch. Roger was wearing that watch one day during one of our walnut wars; he was hiding in the privy behind the weatherboarding as a barrage of black walnuts pelted the side of the privy. I decided to get into the action, and throwing as hard as a six-year-old could, I fired a strike right through a gaping hole in the side of the privy. The walnut hit Roger's wristwatch band and broke it. Needless to say, my bottom received twice the damage from Roger and Mother—far worse than the one strike I threw with a black walnut.

Before Roger went into the navy, he would keep late hours on the weekends and sleep late in the mornings. Long after the three of us were up, Roger might still be sleeping in the boys' room across the hallway. On one of these occasions, we younger boys got a long string and tied a loop around his big toe, which was sticking out from under the cover. Then we hid across the hallway and jerked as hard as we could, and the chase was on.

As I recall, it was in the winter of 1963 and Mom and Dad had gone to Shreveport, Louisiana, to see Jimmie and Jeanie's new son, J. B., when a winter storm blew in a day or so after Mom and Dad left. The first day of the storm, Bobby promptly stuck the Allis-Chalmers WD tractor when we attempted to feed the cows. The weather was terrible. This was before Bobby and I received our very own electric blankets, and Mom and Dad's room was the only bedroom that had one. Snuggling beneath the covers of this modern marvel was a real treat after such a cold day.

It was around midnight when a loud noise shook the whole house. The front porch roof, which was being held up by pine poles at a forty-five-degree angle, had collapsed. Dad, Bobby and I had been hurriedly attempting to complete the concrete porches beneath the roof when the storm blew in and disaster struck. The weight of the snow and ice snapped the pine poles, and the roof slammed up against the house at the room where Bobby and I were temporarily spending the night. We were sleeping in a four-poster bed Dad had built in 1936. At first neither of us knew what had happened. Every possibility, including an earthquake, went through our minds. It was not until I pulled back the curtains to look out the window did it all come together. Within a foot of my nose and on the other side of the windowpane was a dirt dauber's nest—something usually seen on the underside of the decking of the porch roof. We later demolished the old porch roof and built a new one.

The next year Roger purchased a 1964 Chevrolet Impala and then unexpectedly received orders to Scotland. This caused a small financial crisis for him, since the navy would not ship the car overseas. We still owned the 1950 Chevrolet pickup, but it was a worn-out farm truck. The 1957 Fairlane Ford was seven years old, and Mom and Dad were not ready for a new car. However, Bobby and I were delighted when they took over the payments from Roger; the sporty new car fit right into our youthful plans. It provided a more dependable commute for Bobby to the university and to Mother's work at Five Points in Athens.

Dad was in great need of a newer pickup truck. But it would be later on, after all the boys were out of the nest, when the income from two chicken houses could provide enough cash for him to buy one.

1963

Mom, Dad, and Me

Out of the Nest

❦ ———— ❧

R oger left home for the navy in 1957, but he still had his eye on a certain girlfriend back home in Watkinsville. He married Sonia Huff in 1959, and the two of them would go wherever the navy sent them. They were in Astoria, Oregon, when Dad came to the boys' room one morning in 1960 and said, "Uncle Jim, Uncle Bob, and Uncle Bill, it's time to get up!" And so it was that our first nephew, Ricky, was born. Roger spent twenty years in the United States Navy and became a nuclear component welder and a chief petty officer hull technician.

In 1961, Jimmie joined the air force and rapidly attained rank to E-9. He served in Thailand during the Vietnam War and later became the senior enlisted advisor for the Alaskan Air Command. While serving in Southern California, he received a master's degree in international relations from the University of Southern California. He spent his last tour of duty at Montgomery Air Force Base, overseeing a large staff of enlisted journalists writing curricula for air force recruits. He returned home in 1990, after twenty-nine years of active service.

The year 1961 was another pivotal one for the rest of the family at home. Phillip and Ralph died within a few months of each other, leaving the inheritance issues in a tumultuous state of affairs. Between

Phillip's five original children, his two children by Sara Martin, and the grandchildren they all produced, it's easy to see how confusing these issues became. Ultimately our family was given the option to purchase the Vandiver place and the forty-one-acre Holbrook farm. A significant number of those families' heirs doubted Mom and Dad could pay for the two nearby farms. However, a personal contact through the family attorney provided Mom and Dad a temporary loan, and we became the owners of 160 acres of prime farmland. The final decree in Phillip's will also made his grandchildren heirs to a five-hundred-acre tract of timberland in Apalachee, Georgia, with the stipulation that they could not inherit it until twenty years after his death.

Dad could access the Vandiver farm from Kirkland Road, but it was still a long drive back to where the Vandiver house was located beneath a stand of large oak trees. I can only try to express the absolute joy I experienced living on the same forty-one-acre tract that was once owned by my great-great-grandparents. Many times I have walked to the 120 acres just down Kirkland Road to the 120 acres my great-grandparents had owned and where my mother and her family once lived. In the 1960s, as a teen growing up in Oconee County, I was very privileged to work, live, and hunt on the same land my ancestors had owned. It was prime for small-game hunting and deer hunting, and that suited me just fine.

I was eleven years old when we purchased the farm, and before the deal went through, I had overheard talk of us having to move from the Hardigree-Holbrook house. I could not get my mind around that idea. After the purchase, Mother and Dad celebrated with a supper of oyster stew. As they prepared supper, they still were talking over my head about how it had all come about. The only thing I wanted to know was whether or not we had to move. I remember the relief I felt when Dad put his arm around me and said, "No, we're not going anywhere." Soon a representative from the Farm Home Administration came to our house and recommended that Dad borrow enough money to build a poultry house and pay off the temporary loan. Dad took his advice, and little by little, things began to improve financially. With this better life, we were back to the farming grind more than ever, just to be able to afford it.

Dad was most interested in the acreage for row-cropping purposes; the terraces that had been thrown in the past decades by mule and plow were still in place, grown over with different species of saplings, including sugarberries. In the off-season we would start at the Kirkland Road entrance and work our way over the entire acreage, clearing off those saplings with a long chain, tongs, and a tractor. Sometimes Dad would use dynamite to blast off the roots of a tough sugarberry bush, and sometimes even a bulldozer would be brought in to accomplish what a farmer, his sons, and an Allis-Chalmers WD tractor could not do. Dad had some of the most restful and enjoyable experiences of his life nestled down behind the steering wheel of his truck, watching a D8 bulldozer change the face of the earth. He paid dearly for it, but nothing in the world was more pleasurable for him to watch than this type of hired work.

Bobby and I rode the school bus and came home after school to farm chores and home improvements. During this period, Bobby and I became handy with a hammer and crowbar—not for building, necessarily, but for the destruction of nearly a dozen outbuildings that had become eyesores. This work was done in conjunction with our day-to-day farm chores.

Bobby's goals were set for a college education, and in the fall of 1963, he left for Americus, Georgia, to attend Georgia Southwestern Junior College. I can still feel the loneliness I experienced at age thirteen, with the big upstairs left all to myself. I was not ignorant of the workload that now rested on Dad and me. Most of the time after school I would eat a snack and then join Dad at whatever he was doing that day. Sometimes that meant going straight to the fields, but most of the time the routine farm chores were always waiting. In 1963, my driving was limited to the cultivation field, but when President Kennedy was assassinated, I was allowed to drive three miles to the Howard Ward place to notify Dad.

Every day we fed 11,500 chickens by carrying two five-gallon feed buckets, twice, to each of forty feed troughs in the poultry house.

When this was finished, there were five cows to milk and the hogs to be fed. Soon Dad built a second poultry house, but it was equipped with automatic feeders, something both houses eventually received. Poultry became the cash crop for the family, and our row cropping waned as the equipment began to wear out and Dad approached retirement age.

The apple did not fall too far from the tree when it came to the work ethic my dad practiced and therefore instilled in me. I enjoyed the physicality and the laborious nature of my chores. I could see and feel my body developing and changing by the month; I went from being five feet tall in 1963, at age thirteen, to six feet tall and 185 pounds by 1968. These were the only years of my life that I can remember maintaining the proper body-mass index, and that fact was attributable to farm work.

In 1965, Bobby transferred to the University of Georgia, commuting to Athens with Mother each day until his graduation in 1968, the same year I graduated from high school. Vietnam and the draft were somewhat synonymous and required our patriotic attention. Bobby was placed in a deferred classification due to a kidney ailment, and I joined the navy.

With a degree in business administration, Bobby worked as an assistant manager at a department store for a while but moved on to City Service Oil Co-Op, and ultimately went into banking when he moved to Tulsa, Oklahoma. (He was the first banker to place an ATM in Tulsa.) He contracted with the Resolution Trust Cooperation for a while after the Whitewater scandal, and afterward he went into business with the Edward Jones Financial Group, of which he is now part owner.

For all the years my elder brothers were at home, our family's farming routine was relatively the same; thus the chores and work were the same. However, by 1965, diversified methods of farming were required to secure loan payments, and so Dad incorporated poultry, row cropping, and cattle into the farming routine. The work now fell primarily upon the shoulders of my Dad and me. My social life at school was all but nonexistent, but Dad realized I needed some "me time," and I was allowed to hunt and fish and spend time with my closest friends.

The year 1965 was an eventful one, for that's when I received the Future Farmers of America State Home Improvement Award and won a trip to the National FFA Convention in Kansas City, Missouri. It was also the year I was introduced to the guitar. My closest friend was John Michael Marable, who was the son of Martha Bell Marable. That fact is significant because the Bells were extremely musically talented, especially when it came to instrumentation. I was impressed with my good friend Mike's musical skill, and soon the two of us were seeking out a means by which I could accompany him. He secured a job for the two of us, peach picking, so I could buy a five-dollar guitar that Mrs. Laura Shelton had been keeping under her bed. Mike and I would practice, marveling at every milestone of our achievement.

Though my dad was amenable to my visiting Mike, he was a bit skeptical of all the time I spent at Mike's house practicing. One evening when I was at Mike's house and needed a ride home, I reluctantly called Mom and Dad for that ride. They, also reluctantly, came for me. To ease the tension, Mike and I put on a miniconcert for both sets of parents. To my surprise, my parents were impressed, and from that moment forward, Mom and Dad became our most avid fans.

Music only added another dimension to the possibilities for my future. By 1969, farming was out of the question and the draft was looming. Mother and Dad wanted me to follow in Bobby's footsteps, but I couldn't see myself doing that. Also, the cost of another college education seemed out of reach for the family and me. I had worked all summer and could barely pay for the fall quarter at a junior college, though I completed it successfully. For financial reasons, I applied to night school at the University of Georgia with an added request for the night school director: if I proved that I could do university work for one quarter, would he allow me into day school as a commuter student? He agreed, but with the condition that I make an A in both courses. I accomplished that benchmark in one of the courses;

however, due to a single error in a single problem in an Accounting 111 test, my hopes of getting a college education were dashed.

That was the hardest academic challenge I experienced until 1977, when the director of the Federal Communications Commission in Atlanta gave me a waiver to take the licensing examination a third and final time. Typically applicants are only allowed to take the licensing examination for a First Class FCC License twice in a six-month period. My employment with Georgia Power and the Southern Company was contingent upon my receiving this license and solidifying my career in telecommunications. This time I was successful.

Though the old Vandiver house had fallen into disrepair by 1968, there was still one room at the front with a viable fireplace, floor, and roof. That's where my friends Mike Marable, Edwin Bowden, and I camped out as their send-off to Vietnam. I soon followed, and in time the three of us became Vietnam veterans. The world has not quite been the same since.

In 1969, given a choice between staying on the farm or going to Vietnam, I would have been perfectly happy to stay and continue the family tradition. But in a long, heart-to-heart conversation, Dad explained to me as best he could that the age of the small farmer in our region was fading into obscurity, and that I should set my goals on a forty-hour workweek.

With help from Bobby, Dad and I farmed the 160-plus acres for nearly ten years. Then, upon my mother's insistence, my parents sold the Vandiver farm to my first cousin Ronnie Hardigree, who at the time was determined to be a farmer. Dad was more than sixty years old and leaning more toward retirement than going $100,000 into debt to buy new farm equipment.

In the spring of 1969, I had only a few months to choose a military branch in which to serve. My best friends, Mike and his cousin Edwin Bowden, had already been drafted and sent straight to Vietnam. Their letters home indicated that they were in a place nobody would want to be, and they persuaded me to avoid being sent there if I could.

I narrowed my choices down to the air force and the navy. When I approached the air force recruiter, he and a subordinate were in a confrontation. Inconspicuously, I stepped into the next doorway down. There sat the navy recruiter with a big smile on his face, welcoming me inside.

When Roger and Jimmie heard that I had joined the navy, they impressed upon me to take seriously the basic battery test that would be given all recruits at a most inopportune time. Usually after traveling from various places from across the country—weary, sleepy, and still in civilian clothes—recruits would be tested in a room full of their peers. The admonition from my brothers echoed in my head as I nodded off from time to time, but I gave it my best. The result was a balanced score across all categories, ranging from 103 to 123. The cutoff for Radioman "A" School was 106. That exact point anchored me in a telecommunications career for the next forty-four years.

After Radioman "A" School, the trainees were asked their preference of orders. The Bureau of Personnel would only consider a preference if radiomen were needed at that duty station. I requested duty with my brother Roger on Guam in the Marianas Islands. To both our surprise, I received orders to the Naval Communications Station, Guam.

Roger and his family preceded my arrival on Guam by several months. Roger was assigned to the USS *Proteus*, a submarine tender near the naval station. I was stationed on the other end of the thirty-mile-long island, near Anderson Air Force Base. For logistical purposes, the Trust Territory of Guam was in a strategic support location for the war effort in Vietnam. On the main island there were several military bases and many military commands within them.

For an interim period of two to three months after arrival, all radio school graduates were kept together on the Naval Communications Station, Guam. During this period, background investigations were completed on all the trainees. I was later told by my family back home that men in black suits were knocking on our neighbors' doors, asking all sorts of questions about my past. Some trainees were cleared for secret and some for top-secret work.

I received a top-secret clearance and was sent to the message center for the commander of naval forces Marianas Islands. The headquarters was located at Top of the Mar, which was an administrative building where the office of President Nixon's brother-in-law, Admiral Pugh, was located.

One afternoon in the summer of 1970, I was being trained on the Auto DIN (Automatic Digital Network), the fastest and highest-capacity system the navy had for interfacing the teletype. Out of this monster spewed perforated paper tape coinciding with incoming messages at a speed of twelve hundred words per minute. It was a state-of-the-art machine, with all the bells and whistles, and alarms for classification and precedence.

All at once the alarm for classification, plus some alarm I had never heard, activated. The communications watch officer heard the commotion and stuck his head into the room to see if I was handling the message appropriately. He knew, in general, what the alarm meant, but he did not want to know specifically what the message contained; then it would be an added responsibility for him. I became weak in the knees when I read the header and saw the TOP SECRET SPECIAL CATEGORY classification from President Nixon at the White House. It was action addressed to his brother-in-law, Admiral Pugh. I thought I should relinquish the message to a higher-ranking and more experienced member of our watch section, but I was instructed by the communications watch officer to gather up the tape, attach it to the mat, make no copies of it, and follow its instruction.

The precedence was Immediate, which meant the message needed to be delivered within thirty minutes. So I did as I was instructed: dressed in my dungaree bell-bottoms, I rode the elevator up four floors to Admiral Pugh's office.

Outside his office was the office of his secretary. When I approached her desk, she asked, "May I help you?"

Gathering together the words that I should say, I was alarmed at what came out of my mouth: "The admiral has a message from the president."

She immediately stood and said, "I'll see if he can see you."

I was thinking, *I sure hope so. I'd be in a heck of a mess if he couldn't.*

To my relief, she immediately returned and said, "He'll see you."

She escorted me into a large office where the admiral sat leafing through papers.

No words were spoken at first as I handed him the message—a bundle of paper tape hanging from a mat—across the large desk where he sat. I stood at parade rest as he silently read the message. When he finished, he handed me the mat and tape and said, "Destroy it."

I popped to attention and said, "Aye, sir!" I then left for the burn room.

On the way to the burn room, I had a couple of things on my mind. One was the extreme contrast between my chore this day and my chores back on the farm. The other was the question of whether I should read the message. Knowing that the message must have been drafted in Washington, DC, I presumed that no more than four or five individuals in the whole world would ever know its contents, and so I read it. From that afternoon until my honorable discharge seven years later, my security clearance was Top Secret Special Category— though it was never used in that capacity again.

The Four Boys

Retirement

❦ —————◉————— ❧

From 1969 until 1998, Mother and Dad had the farm to themselves. Early during this period, they sold the Vandiver place to my first cousin Ronnie Hardigree. They kept the forty-one-acre estate and house that have been the centerpiece of this work. The sale of the Vandiver place, and the final decree of Phillip Hardigree's will, gave them the first glimpse of the kind of life they could only dream of in all their previous years together.

My parents' history with motorized transportation best tells the story of their climb from poverty during the Great Depression to middle-class status. By the time they completed this thirty-year span, there was little evidence of the hardships of their early years together.

Their first vehicle, of course, was the tractor and the platform Dad made for it, reminders of how much easier it was to crank a tractor than to harness a mule. From 1937 to 1947, Dad and Mom primarily borrowed an automobile or caught a ride with a neighbor if they needed to go somewhere. By 1950, their new pickup truck and new Allis-Chalmers WD with farm implements provided the minimum equipment needed to make a crop. By 1957, Mom's employment at the laundry made ours a two-income household; the extra income was enough for the family to afford its first automobile. By coincidence, the 1964 Chevrolet Impala made us a two-car family without the two-car garage. I was fortunate to be able to date in this newer-model car by the late 1960s.

By 1973, Dad had two chicken houses in full operation while Mother was working at Belk in downtown Athens. With our family, as it was with all poultry farmers, the vacation time for trips or excursions always fell between batches of chickens and hatch-out dates. During this time, Dad would make preparations for the next batch of chicks. Depending on the amount of work necessary to prepare for them, he could take a week or even ten days off, if he was fortunate. It was about this time I remember hearing Dad say, "If I'm going to see any of this country before I get too old, I had better get about doing it." At the time, Dad was raising pullets into layers, which took about twenty weeks. So every five months he would get a break.

Dad bought a 1973 long-bed Ford pickup with a camper shell, and Mother still tells of the glorious trips they made through the Delta and the Corn Belt. If it suited them, they would sleep in the camper, but they found it more accommodating to use the camper shell to keep their belongings dry and sleep in the comfort of a motel. And so it was for them during the 1970s—a style of living that had not been possible in all their previous years together.

Mother worked at the laundry for fifteen years and then at Belk for the next eleven, until 1982, for a total of twenty-six years. When it came time for the execution of the final decree of Phillip's will, all of Phillip's grandchildren met and chose Dad and Joe Collier as the executors. Phillip intended for the trees on the tract of timberland to be in prime condition twenty years after his death, and Dad and Joe worked extra hard to get top dollar for it. Each grandchild received his or her portion of a half million dollars with the exception of one, who had requested and received his inheritance earlier, while Phillip was still living. The inheritance enabled Mother to fully retire from Belk. Though Dad wanted a new truck, he wanted even more for Mother to have a car, and they paid cash for a 1982 Thunderbird on the showroom floor. So their trips around the country continued in another new vehicle.

In the early years and during the Depression, when times were hard, Uncle Clarence was always supportive of our family. He would sacrificially give by opening up his clothing store on Sunday afternoons to fit us boys with new suits. He also loaned his automobile to Mom and Dad on numerous occasions. So after their inheritance, Mom and Dad treated themselves, with Uncle Clarence and Aunt Hilda as their guests, to a trip to Daytona Beach in the new car.

Mom and Dad at Daytona

I remember quite clearly the day in the mid-1980s when Dad and I were alone in the second chicken house and I watched him struggle to rise from his one-kneed stance as he worked on an automatic feeder. With disgust, he said, "Bill, I don't think I am going to raise any more chickens."

I said, "If you don't have to, why should you?" At age seventy-six, Dad still had hands that could grip like a vise, and his body still felt like hard rubber, but the arthritis in his joints kept him from being as nimble as he wanted to be to enjoy his work. He and Mother were debt-free, and the time was right for him to cut back on the farming.

From 1961 to 1990, the Hardigree-Holbrook house was in a constant flux with a new roof and another paint job, but the outside looked grand. Dad continued to put his carpentry skills to good use on the inside—lowering the ten-foot ceilings to a standard eight feet, paneling every room, and putting cabinets on every wall in the large kitchen. Dad was very deliberate with his skills; he was determined that Mother would have a comfortable dwelling long after he was gone.

During their earlier years, neither Mom nor Dad had established a sound medical plan that would keep them in good health into retirement. Routine doctor's appointments seemed like a waste of time and money during their middle age. Thus it was impossible for Dad to see how important factors such as blood pressure, blood sugar, and heart rate played into his overall health. From 1988 to 1998, the cumulative effects of two small strokes started Dad down the long road home. To the naked eye, those effects were almost invisible; as doctors became more involved with his health, however, a neurologist told Dad that he had suffered "two mini-strokes." Surprised by his diagnosis, Dad fired back, "I haven't had any!" The doctor chuckled and explained, "*Mini* as in 'small.'"

Mother had her hands full taking Dad to his doctor's appointments during his last decade. She did a splendid job of keeping his medicines straight, for it seemed that every year the doctors would come up with another diagnosis, ranging from type II diabetes to Alzheimer's and Parkinson's to atrial fibrillation. There were moments when

Mother was overwhelmed by the care she provided for Dad. On several occasions, we reassured her that if she remained healthy, the difference between their ages would provide her a life after Dad. Those were very prophetic words.

The exact date and time of Mother's accident are insignificant, but it was a half century later when an old nemesis reappeared. One spring day in 1994, Mother and Dad were burning trash. I don't know whether Dad was confused or just didn't know any better, but he prepared gasoline to start the fire in a fifty-five-gallon barrel. Mother was afraid for Dad to start the fire because of his medical condition, so she stepped in to do the chore. By the time the match was struck and dropped into the drum, the entire space was a bomb waiting to explode. The result was horrific, and the flames engulfed her.

As I had learned in safety training, it is not too much gasoline, but oftentimes too little, that can create an explosion in a confined space. So, like the empty five-gallon can that exploded around the twenty-gallon pot in 1944, killing the "first and last washwoman," a half-century later, an explosion ten times larger was created due to the greater volume of the barrel.

Jimmie was about two hundred yards away, running the tractor, when he looked up and saw Mother rolling in the grass. He quickly called the ambulance.

As I remember, it was late in the afternoon when I walked into my office and my superintendent told me to go to the Athens Regional Hospital emergency room, about seven blocks away. Mother had just arrived and was being attended to. She had not received any pain medicine, although the emergency personnel were working hurriedly to prepare it. She was burned on over 30 percent of her body, on her arms, breasts, stomach, and legs. I remember telling Mom, as she lay there hurting, that they were coming with some "good medicine" for her. Before they transported her to Georgia's burn unit in Augusta, I asked her how she was feeling. She smiled, and this was her reply: "Thank God for that good medicine." Over the next month or so, she received heavy doses of morphine to keep her sedated while they gave her skin grafts from her own body, with a little help from some pigskin.

For all those years before the accident—and with only two of her four boys delivered in a hospital—Mother had taken no more than an aspirin for any ailment. But now her health had reached a fork in the road. She would follow a new road from then on.

Aunt Agnes, Mother's only sister, was so very gracious during Mother's rehabilitation period, coming to live with Dad and Mom for as long as it took for her to get well.

Since 1994, Mother's overall health has been phenomenal. At the risk of providing too much information, she has had a hysterectomy, cataract surgery, gallbladder surgery, and a double knee replacement; received three pacemakers; and had several cancerous skin cells removed. On March 9, 2014, when I relieved her day caretaker, Mother was talking about the time she was run over by the mule-team load of fertilizer. The caretaker, Tonya Williams, exclaimed, "Ms. Ruby, you're like a cat!"

Ms. Ruby Today

Ms. Ruby Today

It was sometime during the mid-1990s, when Mother was approaching her mideighties, that it became clear that the 1982 Thunderbird had run its course. I was honored that she asked me to go with her to purchase her next automobile. From somewhere in her monetary "squirrel holes," she was able to gather the cash for a Dodge Dynasty. However, deciding on that model was not an easy task.

At first I was under the impression that making a $10,000 purchase would provide her with a used modern automobile with all the accessories of the twentieth century. To Mom's credit, she test-drove three vehicles with me and the salesman that day. Each time, I sat in the backseat and the salesman sat in the passenger seat. With each test drive, she downgraded further from buttons, computers, and alarms to the more conventional car like the one she had just retired.

The first automobile she test-drove was quite luxurious, with plenty of space, but I immediately realized she was uncomfortable in it. I reached for the handle above the window for added safety. Her indecision, combined with her age, made the salesman and me uncomfortable. When we hit the bypass around Athens, I thought we would get run over; she simply would not mash the accelerator.

All three of us heaved a sigh of relief when she safely parked the car back on the lot.

I won't say that the salesman was a slow learner, but the second test-drive did not go much better than the first, for it incurred the same results. Mother drove so slowly that we were afraid we would get a ticket for impeding traffic.

But then she sat behind the steering wheel of the front-wheel-drive Dodge Dynasty—a car that was, she noticed, the same model her next-door neighbor, Mrs. Sara M. Downs, drove. When we hit the bypass this time, we hung on for dear life for the opposite reason. She merged into the traffic passing on the left and then on the right. I could see the twinkle in her eye through the rearview mirror. She said, "I think this suits my needs better."

So the tables had turned, but only the salesman and I gave a sigh of relief when she signed on the bottom line and drove it home alone.

All things considered, Mother was truly a good driver. The first time she drove a mechanized vehicle for any length of time was in 1957. She was the primary driver of the Ford Fairlane, which she took to and from work for years at Snow White Laundry. When the 1964 Chevrolet Impala became the family's primary automobile, she drove it for the remainder of her twenty-six years in the "workaday world."

In the close-knit community of Watkinsville in south Oconee County, Georgia, Mother's neighbors and sons would pass her as she zipped by in her Dodge Dynasty. Until age ninety-three, she drove herself to and from all her appointments and any other errands that she might have—not at a speed of twenty or thirty miles an hour, but at the full limit plus five.

This is not to imply that Mother was not gracious in giving up her driving privileges when the time came; quite the contrary. She had seen throughout her life the debacles that her peers, including her own husband, created by driving beyond their years. One such time came in 1992, when Dad sold his last herd bull—an animal weighing more than a ton.

Dad still thought as he had in the past, when it was practical to transport livestock to and from the local livestock barn in a three-quarter-ton pickup. In those years, and to his knowledge, it was adequate to have high bodies on the pickup truck and an accessible chute with which to load any farm animal and haul it to the local sale barn. These bodies Dad made himself. It was like a minifence around the bed of the three-quarter ton pickup. On this particular day in 1992, Dad's huge Hereford bull stepped off the chute into the back of the 1973 three-quarter-ton pickup truck and promptly mashed the tires flat. At the same time, Dad slammed the body door behind the bull. In a flash, the truck's worn shock absorbers became insignificant and the springs were maxed out. Dad immediately left for the livestock barn in Athens, headed down Flat Rock Road with Jimmie and me following close behind. Before Dad made the turn toward Athens from Flat Rock Road, it became apparent that he was driving much too fast. He moved from one lane to the other, while the bull shifted from one side of the pickup to the other. I accelerated and came alongside Dad and told him, "Slow down!" The look on his face is one that I will never forget. He had the most elated, delightful look, grinning from ear to ear. He was obviously enjoying every moment of this last adventure and payday. He did slow down and deliver the bull safely, and the bull brought a good price.

In the late 1990s, Dad's desire to drive his truck became very important to him. But the truck being randomly accessible to him created a real problem. Sometimes Dad would take off down the farm roads, kicking up a dust trail at speeds that were not safe. During a family meeting, it was decided that we should sell the 1973 pickup truck. This was done without Dad's knowledge or consent. When he discovered that his truck had been sold, he legitimately asked, "By whose authority?" adding, "That was my truck!" It was truly sad that his love affair with motorized vehicles had to be so harshly cut short.

The elderly's driving privileges are a legitimate concern for every family. The immediate family has always been the ultimate authority on when those privileges should be taken away. Most often it is a painful but necessary action.

Before our Uncle Carl became a millionaire, he drove every model of Ford, working his way up to the most luxurious models available.

One night after he'd purchased his second Lincoln Continental, he found himself in a tight squeeze in someone's yard, and afterward he boastfully repeated what he had heard the landowner say: "Did you see how many times it took him to turn that Lincoln around?" Not too long after that incident, he rolled his Lincoln up to a friend doing some yard work and parked one of the front wheels on a pile of burning leaves. Later, when the family met to collect his keys, he could not understand why the Lincoln would not stop in his garage. He confused the accelerator for the brake and cut doughnuts in the front yard until he finally found the right pedal.

Mother, on the other hand, even as independent as she has always been, was quite aware of all the eyes that were upon her as her driving skills declined. In some of her last outings when she drove herself, concerned people would approach her and ask her if she needed help. "I must have looked like I shouldn't be driving," she said. Instead of complaining or rebelling, she relinquished her driving privileges and has become a chauffeured queen of gracious living.

Except for Dad's passing, the family has been blessed with excellent health. The remaining five of us are still living our lives as fully as we can afford to do it. Our ages range from sixty-four to ninety-six. Mother, Roger, and I are fully retired, and Jimmie and Bobby are semiretired and working only because they enjoy it.

With the exception of Bobby, who is part owner of Edward Jones and lives in Tulsa, the rest of the boys still live in the Watkinsville area. Our function as family members is to rotate every third night, relieving Mother's daytime caretakers. Callie Watson sits with Mom from nine to five Monday through Friday, and Tonya Williams stays nine to five on the weekends. The job description for all us boys is to heat and serve the delicious meals that Callie has already cooked, wash and dry the dishes, and take out the garbage. The day caretakers wash clothes, clean house, and help with Mom's personal hygiene. When she's not sitting on the front or back screened porch, she is entertained by the big-screen television Bob provided for her, especially when *The Waltons*, Marty Stuart, *Hee Haw*, *The Cumberland Highlanders*, Andy Griffith, Bill Gaither, and others come on at their regularly scheduled times.

For the past two years, the five of us have kept Mother happy and healthy at home. That is the most important thing we all do. Roger contracted the work for building a wheelchair ramp in and out of Mother's house. Though she does not need a wheelchair, it has made accessibility much easier. Jimmie spent almost thirty years away from home, but his actions since he retired from the air force have proven where his heart was during his career. He has been quite the handyman around the home and has kept up the yards, landscaping, and house maintenance.

The night helpers sleep on a foldout bed in the hallway just outside Mom's bedroom, in case she should need anything during the night. One of the reasons this operation works so efficiently is the financial help from Bobby, whose separation from us by the miles does not diminish his charity. He and his wife, Gigi, come home several times a year, and the red carpet is rolled out for everyone.

The big house was made cozy by all the work Dad put in to improve it during his latter years. The improvements, which are still apparent today, are a testament to the love he had for his family. It set the precedent for how he wanted the rest of the family to conduct themselves in his absence. That type of love continues today and is obvious in all those who care for Ms. Ruby. All of us who care for her also love one another, and we are not ashamed to express it.

As often as I can when it is my night, I try to grab both Mother's hands and pull her up from her chair when she has to get up. It is an opportunity to give her a standing hug and tell her I love her. She always reciprocates, saying, "I love you too."

One evening she added this comment: "I'm getting attached to you boys."

I said, "Well, isn't that the way it's supposed to be with your immediate family?"

She replied, "I mean, especially now."

Room 6117

❦ ——— ⟡ ——— ❦

The time for the Antioch Revival and the annual barbecue had rolled around once again. It was August 9, 2014, and my turn to sit with Mother. Her appetite seemed to be falling off as she sat at the supper table, stirring the pork barbecue around on her plate. As in times past, this behavior was not alarming. Her appetite tended to come and go.

When I sat with her again on August 11, I noticed that she was very restless and moved incessantly, more so than any time in the previous two years. This was a significant change. I was afraid she would become exhausted and collapse to the floor; a broken bone would hasten her demise. At two in the morning, she was sick with the dry heaves, and I called the Athens Regional Medical Center's emergency room. They were having a slow night, so I loaded Mother into my pickup truck and took her there. Tests determined she had low blood sodium, and she was given a diagnosis of hyponatremia. She was admitted and put in room 6117, near the nurse's station. The IVs that were administered also caused her to retain fluid, so after five days she was sent home with oral diuretics to gradually remove the twenty pounds that had been added to her baseline weight of 161 pounds.

Room 5136

M other returned home for a week or two that August, but her health was at a critical balance. Except for her splendid mind, the rest of her ninety-six-year-old body was performing marginally. The inverse relationship between her heart medications and her kidney medications and other organs was the focus of her six caretakers. A healthy balance was impossible to maintain. Her mobility dwindled to half of what it was just a month earlier. Her appetite seemed to be reduced by half too.

Mother had struggled with chronic kidney disease for fourteen years. Early in 2014, she'd decided to forego dialysis simply because of the hardship it would place upon her and her caretakers. By August, her second pacemaker would be viable for only three more months. Her heart murmur and arrhythmia had a part to play in her declining health.

Her shortness of breath was brought about by increased fluid retention; fluid retention was brought about by poor heart and kidney function. On August 31, the restlessness that was a side effect of the increasing congestive heart failure caused her to be hospitalized for the second time in the same month. The doctors were very kind to her and the family as they explained the parameters of the narrow road she would have to walk.

The head cardiologist, Dr. Robert Sinyard, told Jimmie, "We are in a tight spot."

Hospice at Home

Mother was transferred from Athens Regional Medical Center to hospice at home. The entire family of five was present during her transfer and the introduction into this final phase of her life. There would be no more hospitalizations for Mother's condition. Hospice and her caretakers would handle all her needs henceforth.

We can never choose how we leave this life. Though the rest of Mother's body was operating only marginally, her splendid mind never failed her. Only she could have said whether it was a blessing or a curse as the "tight spot" closed in on her. With a clear mind she saw it coming. Mother was dying. The Hardigree-Holbrook house had become a five-star convalescent home, with loving individuals caring for her around the clock. For a half century it was Dad's final residence, with Mother as his caretaker. For sixty-four years, Mother lived at the same address. As the bitter winter days hold on just before spring, so did Mother hold tightly to the will to live.

Aided by comfort medication, Mother's last night came on October 23, 2014. I was with her, following the nurse's instructions to keep her comfortable.

Mother passed away at ten the next morning on October 24, 2014, in the arms of Callie Watson, her beloved attendant.

Bibliography

Elder, Ernest. *The Elder Hardigree Book.*

Halbert's Family Heritage. *The World Book of Lavenders.*

Wilson, G. J. N. *The Early History of Jackson County, Georgia.*

The Oconee Enterprise. August 29, 1974.

Ward, Roy. *A Little Black Book of Joy and Sorrow.*

Reed, T. W. "Mob Lynching 1905." *Atlanta Constitution.*

Wilkes, D. "Lynchings in Clarke and Oconee Counties." Paper.

The Atlanta Journal. Special Dispatch. May 5–31, 1905.

Doster, Gary L. Notes.

Welles, Orson. *The War of the Worlds.* 1938.

The Lavenders of Amherst.

Lavender, Billy Boyd. *A Pioneer Church in the Oconee Territory.*

Clark, Josh. Web page on mitochondrial DNA.

News.NationalGeographic.com

Griffiths, Our Kin.

Duffy, Laura Beth. *Native Genealogy.*

History of the Navy Supply Corps School (Normal Town).

The Booth Book.

Ancestry.com.

Notes by Vernon and Millie.

About the Author

Billy Boyd Lavender first discovered his love for writing while serving as a radioman in the US Navy (1969–1977). In this field, accuracy was essential for ship-to-shore communication. He then easily transitioned from the teletype to the computer and published works. He resides in Watkinsville, Georgia.

Printed in the United States
By Bookmasters